Exploring India's Industrial Giants

Exploring India's Industrial Giants

Past & Present

Olivia k

UNIEK ENTERPRISES

CONTENTS

INDEX

Chapter 1: Introduction
1.1 Introduction to the theme of the book.
1.2 Brief overview of India's historical industrial landscape.
1.3 Significance of exploring India's industrial giants.

Chapter 2: Historical Foundations
2.1 Delve into India's historical cottage industries.
2.2 Influence of ancient textile trade and craftsmanship.
2.3 Impact of the East India Company and colonial-era industries.

Chapter 3: The Age of Public Enterprises
3.1 Examination of the role of public sector giants in post-independence India.
3.2 key public enterprises such as SAIL, BHEL, and IOC.
3.3 Contributions to infrastructure development and economic growth.

Chapter 4: The IT Revolution
4.1 Exploration of the IT industry's emergence in India.
4.2 Profiles of IT giants like TCS, Infosys, and Wipro.
4.3 The role of IT in shaping India's digital and economic future
.

Chapter 5: Contemporary Industrial Titans
5.1 In-depth look at modern industrial giants like Reliance Industries and the Adani Group.
5.2 Their diversified interests and contributions to various sectors.
5.3 Their role in driving innovation, employment, and economic growth.

Chapter 6: Pharma and Healthcare Powerhouses
6.1 Analysis of India's pharmaceutical industry and key players.
6.2 Contributions to global healthcare and accessibility.
6.3 Focus on companies like Sun Pharmaceutical and Dr. Reddy's Laboratories.

Chapter 7: The Automotive Sector

7.1 Spotlight on India's automotive industry, with a focus on Tata Motors and Mahindra & Mahindra.

7.2 Evolution of the sector and adaptation to changing trends.

7.3 Influence on the domestic and global automotive market.

Chapter 8: The Future of India's Industrial Giants

8.1 Discussion of the future prospects and challenges facing India's industrial giants.

8.2 Potential for continued growth, innovation, and global impact.

8.3 Closing thoughts on the dynamic evolution of India's industrial landscape.

Chapter 1

Introduction

India's financial excursion is a story of change, development, and versatility. Throughout the long term, this different and dynamic country has seen the ascent and development of modern goliaths that have formed not exclusively its own predetermination however have additionally made a permanent imprint on the worldwide monetary scene. In "Investigating India's Modern Monsters: Past and Present," we set out on a convincing investigation of this unprecedented excursion, divulging the tales of these goliaths, their verifiable importance, and their contemporary pertinence.

The subcontinent of India, with its rich social embroidery and old practices, has a background marked by craftsmanship and exchange that goes back centuries. From the complicatedly woven materials of old India, pursued by vendors and merchants from around the world, to the nearby craftsman's perplexing ceramics and the smith's talented fashioning of metal apparatuses, India's commitment to early modern and monetary exercises was significant. The bungalow businesses of India, which delivered a wide exhibit of merchandise inside families and little studios, played an essential job in the country's monetary legacy.

These enterprises took special care of nearby and provincial business sectors as well as participated in exchange with far off lands.

The authentic meaning of India's material industry is especially essential. The specialty of winding around and texture creation, finely woven into the embroidered artwork of Indian history, was praised for its craftsmanship and quality. Indian cotton and silk textures tracked down their approach to business sectors as distant the Roman Realm, exhibiting the amazing aptitude of Indian craftsmans. The well established customs of material creation bear demonstration of the foundations of India's modern ability and its initial associations with worldwide exchange organizations.

Be that as it may, the direction of India's modern process took a huge turn during the time of English pioneer rule. The East India Organization, with its royal desires, achieved a progression of changes that would lay the preparation for present day industrialization. This period saw the rise of ventures, for example, jute plants, coal mining, and railroad foundation, which planned to serve the interests of the pilgrim organization. The impact of the English frontier presence was permanent, and the improvement of modern foundation, combined with the double-dealing of India's assets, assumed a critical part in India's possible walk toward industrialization.

The meaning of these verifiable establishments couldn't possibly be more significant. The tradition of the pioneer period left a profound effect on India's monetary and modern scene. It laid the foundation for the coordination of India into the worldwide economy, while at the same time delivering different difficulties that would should be defeated in the years to come. The progress from a to a great extent agrarian and high quality society to a beginning modern force to be reckoned with was a mind boggling process, set apart by financial and social changes that have resounded through time.

Post-freedom, India set out on another way of monetary turn of events and independence. One of the critical elements of this post-freedom time was the focal pretended by the public area in forming the country's modern scene. The public authority's contribution in key areas, like steel creation, weighty designing, and petrol, prompted the foundation of public area goliaths that contributed fundamentally to framework improvement and the country's monetary advancement.

Steel Authority of India Restricted (SAIL), Bharat Weighty Electricals Restricted (BHEL), and Indian Oil Company (IOC), among others, assumed significant parts in building the fundamental modern framework of India. These public endeavors, with their tremendous creation abilities and vital significance, were instrumental in the country's quest for confidence and independence.

The introduction of the data innovation (IT) industry in India denoted a significant defining moment in the country's modern development. The late twentieth century saw the rise of IT monsters like Goodbye Consultancy Administrations (TCS), Infosys, and Wipro, which spearheaded another time of financial development and mechanical advancement. These organizations tackled India's talented labor force and upper hand in the worldwide IT administrations market to push the country to the very front of the advanced age.

The IT business' fast development achieved massive changes in the manner business was directed, both inside India and on a worldwide scale. India became known as a center for IT reevaluating and programming improvement, drawing in global clients looking for savvy, top notch arrangements. This momentous change in the modern scene cultivated monetary development as well as generally modified the work scene, making another age of IT experts who were fundamental to the worldwide economy.

The juncture of verifiable establishments, post-freedom industrialization, and the IT upset lays out a convincing representation of India's modern past. It is a set of experiences described by strength, transformation, and the quest for monetary development. Nonetheless, the account of India's modern monsters doesn't end here.

In the contemporary modern scene, India is home to another age of modern monsters that have differentiated their inclinations and extended their impact across different areas. Organizations like Dependence Ventures, drove by Mukesh Ambani, have advanced into diverse combinations, taking part in petrochemicals, broadcast communications, and retail. The Adani Gathering, under the initiative of Gautam Adani, has turned into a central part in areas like framework, environmentally friendly power, and strategies. These modern goliaths are driving advancement, business, and monetary development, both in India and on the worldwide stage.

The drug business is one more urgent area in India's modern scene. Organizations like Sun Drug Enterprises and Dr. Reddy's Research facilities have made huge commitments to worldwide medical care. India's drug industry assumes a urgent part in giving reasonable and open meds to individuals around the world, making medical services more available and reasonable.

The auto area, as well, stands firm on a noticeable foothold in India's modern scene. Organizations like Goodbye Engines and Mahindra and Mahindra have been central members, delivering many vehicles from traveler vehicles to business trucks. Their versatility in light of changing customer inclinations and worldwide ecological principles shows the business' flexibility and obligation to advancement.

As India keeps on stating its presence on the worldwide modern stage, the impact of these contemporary goliaths stretches out past the public lines. The effect of these modern chiefs rises above financial development; it influences advancement, maintainability, and worldwide exchange. Their commitments are demonstrative of the dynamic and always developing nature of India's modern scene.

1.1 Introduction to the theme of the book.

The subject of this book is an investigation of the exceptional excursion of India's modern monsters, over a significant time span. A story takes us through the complexities of a country's monetary development, featuring the significant effect of these modern forces to be reckoned with on the nation's set of experiences, culture, and the worldwide economy. India, a place where there is old practices, momentous craftsmanship, and a rich verifiable embroidery, has seen a different scope of enterprises that have molded its fate and its job in the world-wide monetary scene.

The tale of India's modern goliaths is one of getting through change, variation, and development. A story of versatility traverses hundreds of years, from the hour of old bungalow businesses to the rise of current combinations.

The account winds through the strings of India's set of experiences, uncovering how early bungalow businesses, with their high quality customs, established the groundwork for the huge modern scene we witness today.

The underlying foundations of India's modern process can be followed back to the bungalow businesses that flourished in the sub-continent for quite a long time. These were limited scale, decentralized types of creation where products were made inside individual families or nearby studios. These cabin enterprises played an essential job in gathering the fundamental necessities of people and networks while adding to nearby exchange and local monetary organizations.

One of the eminent parts of India's verifiable modern scene was its lively material industry. The textures created in India were praised for their complicated craftsmanship, quality, and one of a kind plans. Indian materials tracked down their direction to far off business sectors, including the Roman Realm, filling in as a demonstration of the skill and imagination of Indian craftsmans. The house business of material creation had a huge effect on the neighborhood economy as well as on the country's worldwide exchange organizations.

The verifiable meaning of India's material industry is a demonstration of the country's striking skill in craftsmanship and exchange. The perplexing system of turning, winding around, and coloring was given over through ages, with families or neighborhood societies safeguarding and refining their strategies. The textures delivered bore remarkable provincial attributes and plans, mirroring the assorted societies and characters of various pieces of India. This rich and different social woven artwork has characterized India's modern legacy.

Be that as it may, the direction of India's modern process took a significant turn during the time of English pilgrim rule. The appearance of the East India Organization denoted a time of tremendous change in the country's financial scene. The pioneer organization presented English modern practices and advances, which prompted the foundation of ventures, for example, jute plants, coal mining, and rail line framework. These improvements laid the basis for current industrialization, making an extension from India's verifiable establishments to its modern future.

The tradition of the English pioneer presence in India made a permanent imprint on the country's modern scene. It was a period set apart by the double-dealing of India's assets and the improvement of modern foundation to serve the interests of the pilgrim organization. The time saw the rise of enterprises that were decisively intended to serve the requirements of the English Domain while likewise having extensive ramifications for India's own modern turn of events.

The shift from an agrarian and high quality society to an arising modern country was a mind boggling and complex interaction. While the frontier time achieved huge modern changes, it likewise introduced difficulties and financial abberations that would should be tended to in the post-freedom period. The change to current industrialization would require a thorough comprehension of the effect of English expansionism and the assurance to beat the difficulties it presented.

Post-freedom, India set out on another way of monetary turn of events, looking for independence and financial development. The post-freedom time was portrayed by the focal pretended by the public area in forming the country's modern scene. The public authority's contribution in key areas, like steel creation, weighty designing, and oil, prompted the foundation of public area goliaths that assumed significant parts in framework improvement and the country's monetary advancement.

Steel Authority of India Restricted (SAIL), Bharat Weighty Electricals Restricted (BHEL), and Indian Oil Company (IOC), among others, were at the front of building India's modern foundation. These public endeavors, with their tremendous creation abilities and key significance, were instrumental in the country's quest for confidence and independence. They assumed basic parts in foundation advancement, energy creation, and transportation, adding to the country's monetary development and soundness.

The development of these public area goliaths denoted a huge stage in India's modern development. These ventures were basic to the country's turn of events, and they assumed a significant part in molding the country's financial scene in the post-freedom period. The progress to present day industrialization and independence required the planned endeavors of these public area substances and the country's obligation to its own development.

One of the pivotal occasions in India's modern process was the development of the data innovation (IT) industry. The late twentieth century saw the ascent of IT monsters like Goodbye Consultancy Administrations (TCS), Infosys, and Wipro, which drove India into another period of monetary development and mechanical advancement. These organizations outfit India's gifted labor force and upper hand in the worldwide IT administrations market to push the country to the very front of the computerized age.

The IT business' fast development cultivated financial extension as well as achieved basic changes in the manner business was led both inside India and on a worldwide scale. India became eminent as a center point for IT rethinking and programming improvement, drawing in global clients looking for savvy, top notch arrangements. This change of the modern scene prompted the formation of another age of IT experts who assumed a pivotal part in the worldwide economy.

The combination of verifiable establishments, post-freedom industrialization, and the IT unrest illustrates India's modern past. It is a set of experiences set apart by flexibility, variation, and the quest for monetary development. However, the narrative of India's modern goliaths doesn't finish up here.

In the contemporary modern scene, India is home to another age of modern monsters that have differentiated their inclinations and extended their impact across different areas. Organizations like Dependence Ventures, drove by Mukesh Ambani, have developed into diverse combinations, participating in petrochemicals, broadcast communications, and retail. The Adani Gathering, under the authority of Gautam Adani, has turned into a central part in areas like foundation, environmentally friendly power, and planned operations. These modern goliaths are driving advancement, work, and financial development, both in India and on the worldwide stage.

The drug business is one more urgent area in India's modern scene. Organizations like Sun Drug Ventures and Dr. Reddy's Research centers have made huge commitments to worldwide medical services. India's drug industry assumes an essential part in giving reasonable and open meds to individuals around the world, making medical services more available and reasonable.

The car area, as well, stands firm on an unmistakable foothold in India's modern scene. Organizations like Goodbye Engines and Mahindra and Mahindra have been central members, delivering a large number of vehicles from traveler vehicles to business trucks. Their flexibility in light of changing buyer inclinations and worldwide natural guidelines exhibits the business' strength and obligation to advancement.

As India keeps on stating its presence on the worldwide modern stage, the impact of these contemporary monsters stretches out past the public lines. The effect of these modern chiefs rises above financial development; it influences advancement, maintainability, and worldwide exchange. Their commitments are demonstrative of the dynamic and always developing nature of India's modern scene.

All in all, "Investigating India's Modern Monsters: Past and Present" leaves on an enamoring venture through India's modern history, uncovering the striking changes, difficulties, and victories that have portrayed the country's financial development. From the old material merchants to the advanced IT and computerized pioneers, from the time of public area goliaths to the broadened aggregates of today, this investigation enlightens India's modern process, its authentic roots, and its persevering through significance in the worldwide monetary scene. This book is an encouragement to uncover the accounts of the visionaries, trend-setters, and pioneers who have added to India's modern inheritance and keep on forming its promising future. It is a demonstration of India's soul of versatility, flexibility, and its consistently developing mission for financial development and progress.

1.2 Brief overview of India's historical industrial landscape.

India's verifiable modern scene is an embroidery woven with the strings of hundreds of years of craftsmanship, exchange, and financial development. This outline plans to give bits of knowledge into the assorted and rich legacy of India's modern history, following its foundations from the bungalow enterprises of old times to the rise of current modern goliaths.

The narrative of India's modern scene is unpredictably associated with its dynamic custom of cabin businesses. These limited scale, decentralized types of creation included the formation of merchandise inside individual families or neighborhood studios. These house ventures were instrumental in gathering the fundamental necessities of people and networks, adding to neighborhood exchange, and laying out provincial monetary organizations.

One of the most striking parts of India's verifiable modern scene was its rich material industry. The specialty of winding around and texture creation was commended for its craftsmanship, quality, and novel plans. India's cotton and silk materials were exceptionally pursued by shippers and brokers from around the world, tracking down their direction into business sectors as far off as the Roman Realm. The bungalow business of material creation was critical for nearby exchange as well as assumed an essential part in the country's initial associations with worldwide exchange organizations.

The antiquated customs of turning, winding around, and coloring were gone down through ages, with families and nearby societies safeguarding and refining their procedures. Subsequently, the textures created bore interesting provincial attributes and plans, mirroring the assorted societies and characters of various pieces of India. This rich and various social embroidered artwork was necessary to characterizing India's modern legacy.

The verifiable meaning of India's material industry is apparent in the complexities of the specialty, with every district of India contributing its exceptional plans and strategies. From the dynamic shades of Rajasthan's block-printed materials to the fragile handwoven silks of Varanasi, India's material legacy is a demonstration of the innovativeness and abilities of its craftsmans. The material exchange was a wellspring of monetary movement as well as a social trade, as textures conveyed with them the narratives, customs, and characters of the districts from which they began.

Regardless of the predominance of material creation in India's initial modern scene, other house ventures were likewise flourishing. Stoneware, metalwork, and carpentry were among the specialties that altogether affected nearby economies and social customs. These specialties were in many cases profoundly implanted in the day to day routines of individuals, filling both utilitarian and tasteful needs. The craftspeople, frequently coordinated into neighborhood societies or networks, invested heavily in their abilities, safeguarding and passing down their insight through ages.

The bungalow businesses assumed a crucial part in giving jobs to a significant piece of the populace, particularly in agrarian social orders. Much of the time, these enterprises were entwined with horticultural cycles, as ranchers and rustic families took part in material creation, ceramics making, or different artworks during agrarian slow times of year. This valuable pay filled in as a cushion against the dangers related with cultivating, guaranteeing a level of financial strength for rustic families.

Cabin ventures additionally offered adaptability and flexibility, empowering people to offset their occupations with different obligations. For instance, ladies often participated in cabin businesses like winding around and turning, permitting them to add to their families' pay while overseeing homegrown obligations. These enterprises, implanted in the texture of regular daily existence, contributed not exclusively to monetary prosperity yet in addition to social union and local area bonds.

The financial meaning of bungalow enterprises stretched out past individual families. The deal and trade of merchandise delivered by these enterprises frequently framed the premise of nearby and provincial exchange organizations. Towns and towns became focuses of creation and exchange, making monetary interdependencies and reinforcing local area bonds. The interconnectedness of cabin enterprises added to the social and monetary texture of nearby networks, cultivating participation and common help.

The conservation and transmission of social legacy were fundamental to India's cabin enterprises. Customary craftsmanship was gone down through ages, with families or neighborhood societies keeping up with and refining their strategies. Apprenticeships and casual learning were normal, guaranteeing the congruity of information and expertise move across ages. The safeguarding of these customary abilities stays a fundamental part of cabin ventures today.

The coming of huge scope industrialization during the eighteenth and nineteenth hundreds of years carried tremendous changes to India's monetary scene. Modern plants, automation, and large scale manufacturing arose, supplanting or changing numerous bungalow enterprises. While the shift to huge scope modern creation was driven by mechanical headways and the quest for more prominent productivity, it additionally introduced new open doors and difficulties.

The change from cabin businesses to enormous scope industrialization made a few significant impacts. From one perspective, it expanded the creation limit and result of merchandise, adding to financial development and the ascent of shopper culture. Efficiently manufactured things turned out to be more reasonable and open, prompting enhancements in expectations for everyday comforts for some.

Then again, the shift to industrialization likewise introduced difficulties. Plant work frequently expected workers to pass on their homes and move to metropolitan focuses, disturbing laid out examples of life and local area.

The division of work in manufacturing plants decreased laborers' jobs to explicit, monotonous assignments, as opposed to the different and complex jobs they frequently played in bungalow ventures. Work conditions in processing plants were once in a while unforgiving, and worries about laborers' freedoms and prosperity arose.

The change to industrialization had significant social, monetary, and social ramifications. It denoted the conclusion of an important time period described by limited scope, decentralized creation and the start of another stage in India's modern history. While the shift achieved tremendous changes, it didn't proclaim the finish of bungalow enterprises.

In many areas of the planet, limited scope, locally situated creation endured and, surprisingly, adjusted to the new modern scene. Cabin ventures kept on flourishing in locales where motorized industrialization had not yet completely grabbed hold or where there was an interest for superior grade, hand tailored products. The perseverance of cabin businesses in these settings exhibited their capacity to adjust and advance, displaying their versatility notwithstanding modern change.

The nineteenth century saw the rise of human expression and specialties development, a response to the apparent dehumanization of work in modern plants. Backers of this development advocated the conservation of conventional craftsmanship and the production of carefully assembled, high quality merchandise. This development assumed a part in rejuvenating house enterprises and advancing the worth of high quality items. It accentuated the significance of craftsmanship, quality, and distinction notwithstanding large scale manufacturing.

The resurgence of cabin businesses was not restricted to customary specialties like materials or ceramics; it incorporated a large number of exercises, including food creation, high quality refreshments, and hand tailored cleansers. In the food business, limited scope ranchers and makers of specialty products embraced the standards of house ventures. They focused on the utilization of normal, privately obtained materials and conventional strategies to make one of a kind, excellent items.

The specialty lager industry, for example, saw wonderful development, driven by buyers looking for unmistakable, privately blended drinks. Little specialty breweries could explore different avenues regarding different fixings and blending strategies to make novel flavors and styles, taking care of assorted preferences. The restoration of specialty brew creation turned into an image of the re-visitation of distinctive, hand tailored merchandise that praised quality and independence.

One of the vital qualities of house businesses lies in their capacity to answer quickly to advertise drifts and changing buyer inclinations. These businesses frequently produce little clumps of merchandise, which can be adjusted and redone to satisfy moving purchaser needs.

For instance, the specialty lager industry's prosperity was a demonstration of its capacity to explore different avenues regarding fixings, adjust to arising patterns, and answer different shopper tastes. The powerful idea of bungalow ventures considers adaptability and imagination in fulfilling market needs.

The resurgence of cabin businesses likewise lines up with a more extensive cultural shift toward manageability, privately obtained items, and an emphasis on higher expectations no matter what. Buyers are progressively looking for items with a lower ecological impression, supporting craftsmans and limited scope makers, and esteeming legitimacy and craftsmanship. This reestablished interest in house ventures reflects a social development that values the legacy, custom, and human touch behind the products we consume.

The computerized age plays had a vital impact in the restoration of bungalow enterprises. Online commercial centers and web based business stages have furnished limited scope makers with a worldwide reach, empowering them to interface straightforwardly with buyers.

This computerized change has brought obstructions down to passage for high quality organizations and permitted them to contend in the worldwide commercial center.

1.3 Significance of exploring India's industrial giants.

The investigation of India's modern monsters holds gigantic importance in revealing insight into the country's financial history, progress, and worldwide impact. The narratives of these modern forces to be reckoned with give important experiences into the change of India's modern scene and its job in forming the country's predetermination. This excursion of investigation is a demonstration of India's flexibility, development, and versatility notwithstanding steadily changing financial difficulties.

India's modern goliaths are not simply business substances; they are images of India's monetary advancement. They typify the country's change from a prevalently agrarian culture to a worldwide monetary player. Their accounts are woven into the texture of India's set of experiences, mirroring the intricacies, victories, and difficulties that the nation has encountered all through its excursion towards industrialization.

One of the essential meanings of investigating India's modern goliaths is the acknowledgment of India's verifiable commitments to worldwide exchange and trade. India's house ventures, especially its material exchange, assumed a critical part in associating the country to far off lands, including the Roman Realm. The standing of Indian materials for their perfect craftsmanship, quality, and plan greatness was commended around the world. By investigating this verifiable setting, we gain a more profound appreciation for India's old modern ability and its initial associations with worldwide exchange organizations.

The English frontier period carried tremendous changes to India's modern scene. The East India Organization's strength and the presentation of English modern practices denoted a pivotal stage in India's set of experiences. The foundation of businesses, for example, jute plants, coal mining, and rail line framework not just served the interests of the pilgrim organization yet in addition established the groundwork for current industrialization. The meaning of this pilgrim heritage in molding India's modern future can't be put into words.

Besides, the investigation of India's modern goliaths features the strength of a country that conquered huge difficulties. The progress from house enterprises to huge scope industrialization during the pioneer time was an intricate cycle. While it achieved monetary development and expanded creation limit, it additionally introduced difficulties as far as work conditions and social interruptions. The investigation of this progress highlights India's capacity to adjust to change, safeguard its social and monetary legacy, and construct a more independent modern establishment.

The post-freedom period denoted a critical crossroads in India's set of experiences. The pretended by the public area in molding the country's modern scene was instrumental chasing independence and monetary development. Ventures like Steel Authority of India Restricted (SAIL), Bharat Weighty Electricals Restricted (BHEL), and Indian Oil Company (IOC) became key to foundation advancement and the country's financial advancement. By digging into this time, we gain a more profound comprehension of how India tried to get its financial future and decrease reliance on outer sources.

The development of the data innovation (IT) industry in India denoted an extraordinary stage in the country's modern process. Organizations like Goodbye Consultancy Administrations (TCS), Infosys, and Wipro spearheaded India's entrance into the advanced age. Their prosperity helped India's monetary development as well as put the country at the front of the worldwide IT administrations market. This change mirrors the flexibility and the ability of India's labor force, as well as the upper hands that India could use in the worldwide field.

The investigation of contemporary modern monsters like Dependence Ventures and the Adani Gathering features their capacity to broaden and grow across different areas. These aggregates are currently central parts in petrochemicals, media communications, retail, framework, sustainable power, and strategies. The meaning of these cutting edge goliaths stretches out to driving development, setting out business open doors, and adding to India's financial development on a worldwide scale. This broadening grandstands India's capability to turn into a forerunner in different businesses, upgrading its worldwide impact.

The drug business is another huge area where Indian organizations like Sun Drug Enterprises and Dr. Reddy's Research facilities have made imperative commitments to worldwide medical care. By giving reasonable and open drugs, India's drug industry assumes a urgent part in further developing medical services around the world. The investigation of these organizations underlines the significance of India's part in worldwide wellbeing and admittance to meds.

The auto area likewise assumes a huge part in India's modern scene, with organizations like Goodbye Engines and Mahindra and Mahindra delivering many vehicles. Their capacity to adjust to changing customer inclinations and fulfill worldwide ecological guidelines features the area's commitment to India's monetary development and mechanical advancement.

In the contemporary setting, the meaning of investigating India's modern goliaths lies in the possibility to comprehend what's in store prospects and difficulties confronting the country's modern scene. These goliaths are ready to keep molding India's financial fate and worldwide impact. The illustrations gained from their process can act as significant bits of knowledge for policymakers, business people, and business pioneers as they explore the intricacies of the cutting edge worldwide economy.

Besides, India's modern goliaths have a more extensive worldwide effect. They add to worldwide exchange, venture, and development. Their scope reaches out past public lines, impacting financial elements and exchange relations. As India's modern scene develops, it turns out to be progressively interconnected with the worldwide economy. Understanding the meaning of these monsters assists us with getting a handle on the mind boggling organization of worldwide monetary interdependencies.

The investigation of India's modern monsters likewise stresses the significance of business venture and development in a quickly impacting world. These monsters are results of visionary authority, imaginative reasoning, and an immovable obligation to financial development. Their accounts rouse people in the future of business visionaries and trend-setters, both inside India and all over the planet.

Furthermore, this investigation highlights the basic job that the confidential area plays in molding a country's financial scene. While the public area has generally been critical in India's turn of events, the rise of private modern goliaths shows the powerful idea of India's economy. A flourishing confidential area is imperative for encouraging contest, driving development, and setting out work open doors.

Chapter 2

Historical Foundations

The course of mankind's set of experiences is set apart by a complicated transaction of occasions, thoughts, and people that have formed
the world we occupy today. From the earliest human advancements to
the cutting edge period, the authentic underpinnings of our general
public have been based upon the commitments and clashes of innumer-
able ages. This account means to investigate the key authentic establishments that have laid the basis for the world we know today, analyzing
the ascent and fall of domains, the advancement of political and social
frameworks, the improvement of innovations, and the getting through
tradition of thoughts.

At the beginning of human development, in the prolific waterway
valleys of Mesopotamia and Egypt, the groundworks of coordinated
society were laid. The advancement of horticulture considered the
development of surplus food, which, thus, prompted the ascent of
urban areas and complex social orders. The development of composed
language empowered the recording of regulations, religion, and culture,
giving a way to information to be gone down through ages. In Egypt,
the Nile Stream encouraged a one of a kind connection between

individuals and their current circumstance, as it gave food as well as a feeling of enormous request through yearly flooding. In the mean time, in Mesopotamia, the Tigris and Euphrates waterways were tackled for water system, prompting the development of early city-states like Ur and Uruk.

As social orders advanced, so too did their frameworks of administration. The verifiable groundworks of political association can be followed back to antiquated Mesopotamia, where city-states created particular frameworks of administration. Hammurabi's Code, quite possibly of the earliest known legitimate code, laid out a bunch of regulations and disciplines that mirrored the social and monetary designs of the time. These early general sets of laws were instrumental in molding thoughts of equity and request, and they laid the preparation for the advancement of additional intricate legitimate and political designs in later civilizations.

The old Greeks further added to the authentic groundworks of political idea. In the city-province of Athens, the idea of a majority rule government flourished, permitting residents to take part in dynamic cycles. Figures like Pericles and Solon supported the possibility of municipal investment and law and order. The philosophical insights of Socrates, Plato, and Aristotle gave a philosophical system to political hypothesis, investigating thoughts of equity, morals, and administration. These fundamental thoughts keep on affecting political idea and practice in the advanced world.

The Roman Republic, a development profoundly impacted by Greek idea, offered one more vital layer to the verifiable groundworks of political association. Rome's conservative arrangement of administration, with its partition of abilities and chosen authorities, lastingly affects the advancement of present day majority rule establishments. Besides, the Roman general set of laws, described by the standards of correspondence under the steady gaze of the law and the thought of "ius civile" (common regulation), laid the basis for present day general sets of laws.

The spread of Christianity in the later long periods of the Roman Domain had significant ramifications for the verifiable groundworks of religion, morals, and administration. The lessons of Jesus Christ, as kept in the New Confirmation, presented the ideas of affection, pardoning, and the balance of all devotees to the eyes of God. As Christianity spread across Europe and the Roman Domain deteriorated, the Congregation assumed a focal part in saving information, cultivating schooling, and giving a moral and moral structure for middle age European culture.

Another critical authentic establishment is the Islamic human progress, which prospered during the Medieval times. The Prophet Muhammad's lessons, as kept in the Quran, established the groundworks for another monotheistic religion, Islam. The Islamic Domain extended quickly, enveloping immense regions from Spain to India. Islamic researchers made huge commitments to different fields, including arithmetic, space science, medication, and reasoning. The Place of Shrewdness in Baghdad turned into a focal point of scholarly and logical request, saving and expanding upon the information on prior developments, including the Greeks and Romans.

The European Renaissance, which arose in the fourteenth 100 years, denoted a recovery of traditional learning and established the groundworks for the cutting edge world. Crafted by old Greek and Roman savants, researchers, and craftsmen were rediscovered and embraced. Figures like Leonardo da Vinci, Michelangelo, and Galileo Galilei made critical commitments to craftsmanship and science, making ready for the advanced comprehension of the normal world and the improvement of new imaginative strategies. The Renaissance additionally saw the spread of humanism, accentuating the value and capability of people, and the development of the print machine, which took into consideration the boundless scattering of information.

The time of investigation in the fifteenth and sixteenth hundreds of years denoted a defining moment in world history, as European powers set off to investigate and colonize far off lands.

Christopher Columbus' journeys to the Americas, Vasco da Gama's ocean course to India, and Ferdinand Magellan's circumnavigation of the globe extended the well explored parts of the planet, prompting the trading of merchandise, thoughts, and societies between the Old World and the New World. This period not just established the verifiable starting points for current globalization yet additionally had significant ramifications for native people groups, as their social orders and societies were perpetually modified.

The Illumination, which started in the late seventeenth 100 years and went on into the eighteenth hundred years, further reshaped the authentic underpinnings of thought, legislative issues, and society. Edification masterminds like John Locke, Voltaire, and Jean-Jacques Rousseau pushed for individual privileges, reason, and the detachment of chapel and state. Their thoughts added to the advancement of popularity based beliefs, law and order, and the standards of common freedoms, which keep on molding contemporary political and social frameworks.

Industrialization, which flourished in the late eighteenth 100 years and went on into the nineteenth hundred years, achieved a change in monetary and mechanical establishments. The advancement of steam motors, motorized creation, and new types of transportation upset industry and trade. The authentic groundworks of urbanization and the development of the modern city reshaped social designs and work rehearses. The shift from agrarian social orders to modern economies prompted the ascent of the average workers, the improvement of work developments, and new types of social association.

The nineteenth and mid twentieth hundreds of years were likewise set apart by critical political changes. The spread of patriotism, the downfall of realms, and the ascent of new country states adjusted the political guide of the world. The American Unrest and the resulting development of the US added to the spread of vote based standards and thoughts of self-assurance. In Europe, the Show of Europe looked to keep up with strength following the Napoleonic Conflicts, while patriot developments and the downfall of realms prompted a progression of contentions, including the unrests of 1848 and the unification of Italy and Germany.

The twentieth century carried extraordinary change and commotion to the authentic groundworks of the world. The Second Great War, with its overwhelming human and monetary cost, reshaped the worldwide political scene and denoted the finish of realms. The Russian Upset of 1917 acquainted the world with the philosophy of socialism, which would significantly affect the course of the twentieth hundred years.

The interwar period saw the development of extremist systems, including Adolf Hitler's Nazi Germany and Joseph Stalin's Soviet Association, which dove the world into the bedlam of The Second Great War. The conflict brought about the far and wide annihilation of urban areas, the Holocaust, and the utilization of nuclear weapons in Hiroshima and Nagasaki.

The consequence of The Second Great War prompted the foundation of the Unified Countries and the start of the Virus Battle, as the world wrestled with the philosophical and political divisions between the US and the Soviet Association.

The post-war time frame saw the decolonization of Africa, Asia, and the Center East, as previous settlements acquired freedom and looked to rethink their public characters and political frameworks. The Social liberties Development in the US, alongside hostile to pilgrim developments and freedom battles around the world, featured the significance of social equality and balance. The verifiable underpinnings of common freedoms were additionally hardened with the reception of the General Announcement of Basic liberties by the Assembled Countries in 1948.

The last 50% of the twentieth century brought huge mechanical progressions, especially in the fields of registering and correspondence. The creation of the computer chip and the advancement of the web reformed the manner in which individuals lived and worked, introducing the Data Age. The authentic groundworks of globalization were additionally reinforced as the world turned out to be progressively interconnected through exchange, travel, and the trading of thoughts.

The finish of the Virus Battle in 1991 denoted a huge defining moment in world history. The disintegration of the Soviet Association and the spread of liberal majority rules system appeared to proclaim another period of worldwide collaboration and the victory of free enterprise. Notwithstanding, the 21st century has brought its own arrangement of difficulties and vulnerabilities. The occasions of September 11, 2001, and the ensuing "Battle on Fear" reshaped the worldwide political scene, prompting battles in Afghanistan and Iraq and elevated worries about worldwide security and psychological warfare.

2.1 Delve into India's historical cottage industries.

India's set of experiences is an embroidery of different societies, customs, and financial exercises that have developed over centuries. Among the complex strings that make up this embroidery are the authentic bungalow enterprises that have been the foundation of India's economy for quite a long time. Cabin ventures are limited scale, decentralized, and locally established undertakings that produce a great many merchandise, frequently utilizing conventional techniques and abilities. They play had a huge impact in India's financial and social turn of events, with a rich history that traverses back to old times. This story means to dig into the authentic roots and persevering through importance of India's house businesses.

The verifiable groundworks of India's bungalow businesses can be followed back to the Indus Valley Development, one of the world's earliest metropolitan habitats. Individuals of this antiquated development were talented in stoneware, metallurgy, and material creation. Their dominance of crafted works laid the basis for the future improvement of bungalow businesses in India. Proof of their earthenware, including unpredictably planned earthenware dolls and utensils, mirrors an elevated degree of craftsmanship and creative articulation.

The downfall of the Indus Valley Human progress around 1900 BCE denoted the start of another part in India's set of experiences.

Aryan movement carried with it information on ironworking and the presentation of horticulture, essentially modifying the financial scene. With the spread of farming, individuals of old India started to develop cotton, which would turn into a foundation of the cabin material industry. Cotton cultivating, combined with the specialty of turning and winding around, established the groundwork for the development of bungalow based material creation.

The Maurya and Gupta domains, traversing from the fourth century BCE to the sixth century CE, saw the prospering of different cabin enterprises in India. Material creation and coloring processes, including the utilization of indigo and madder, arrived at a serious level of complexity during this period. The craft of handloom winding, specifically, turned into an indispensable piece of Indian culture. It assumed a crucial part in the improvement of exchange and business, as the interest for Indian materials stretched out past the subcontinent to Southeast Asia, the Center East, and the Mediterranean locale.

The authentic meaning of India's house ventures kept on developing during the middle age time frame, especially during the Mughal Domain (1526-1857). The Mughals were known for their enthusiasm for fine materials and support of craftsmans. Subject to their authority, the craft of weaving, cover winding around, and the creation of complicated metalwork and gems arrived at new levels. The Mughals likewise presented Persian plans and themes, enhancing the stylish variety of India's bungalow industry items. The multifaceted craftsmanship of Indian craftsmans, displayed in the formation of rich materials, pulled in worldwide consideration and exchange. The Mughal time was a brilliant age for India's cabin ventures, denoting a high point in their verifiable development.

One of the most persevering through images of India's verifiable house enterprises is the handloom material area. The handloom business has a rich and complex history that has been complicatedly woven into the texture of Indian culture. Handloom winding around includes the manual production of materials utilizing conventional strategies and methods went down through ages. The business plays had a significant impact in the financial improvement of provincial India, giving work to a large number of weavers and craftsmans.

The variety of handloom customs across various locales of India is a demonstration of the country's social extravagance. Each state and area has its extraordinary winding around methods, plans, and materials. For instance, the Benarasi silk sarees of Varanasi, the Kanjeevaram silk sarees of Tamil Nadu, and the Pashmina cloaks of Kashmir are prestigious for their quality and craftsmanship. These handmade materials have not just characterized the social personalities of their locales however have additionally earned worldwide respect for their imaginative and tasteful worth.

One of the main traits of India's handloom industry is its capacity to adjust and advance. Throughout the long term, it has consumed impacts from various societies and embraced new advancements while safeguarding its customary roots. Handloom weavers keep on utilizing age-old strategies in blend with current hardware, guaranteeing that the cabin business stays applicable in the contemporary world. The Indian government plays likewise had an impact in supporting and advancing handloom weavers through different drives and plans.

One more basic part of India's bungalow enterprises is the development of conventional handiworks. These bungalow enterprises envelop many artworks, including earthenware, metalwork, woodcarving, and gems making. The authentic groundworks of these specialties can be followed back to old times when networks created particular abilities and went them down through ages. These customary handiworks are described by their unpredictable plans, fine specifying, and extraordinary local varieties.

The earthenware and ceramics industry, for example, has a long history in India. Various areas have fostered their unmistakable styles, like the blue earthenware of Rajasthan and the earthenware stoneware of West Bengal. These artworks have both stylish and utilitarian worth and are in many cases a necessary piece of Indian culture and customs.

Metalwork in India has likewise thrived as a bungalow industry for quite a long time. The making of metal ancient rarities, including brassware, bronze models, and mind boggling adornments, requires the abilities of craftsmans who have sharpened their specialty over ages. The many-sided filigree work of Odisha and the Dhokra craft of Chhattisgarh are only a couple of instances of India's rich metalwork legacy.

India's gems making custom is one more huge feature of its house ventures. From resplendent gold and silver adornments to beadwork and gemstone adornments, the variety of plans and styles mirrors the social, territorial, and strict variety of the country. Each piece of gems frequently recounts a story, whether it's an image of a specific local area or a portrayal of strict convictions.

The Indian bungalow industry of gems making has developed over the long run, embracing present day procedures while keeping up with the masterfulness and craftsmanship that make it one of a kind. Craftsmans keep on making pieces utilizing conventional techniques, for example, hand-made filigree and Kundan work, guaranteeing that the authentic underpinnings of this industry stay alive and lively.

One more vital piece of India's cabin enterprises is the conventional craft of hand tailored furnishings. From unpredictably cut wooden seats to extravagantly planned cupboards and tables, the nation has a long history of furniture creation. These pieces frequently feature nearby craftsmanship, with every locale having its interesting style, whether it's the elaborate furniture of Rajasthan or the straightforward, rich plans of Kerala.

Carpentry methods have been gone down through ages, safeguarding the verifiable underpinnings of India's house furniture industry. Craftsmans invest wholeheartedly in their work, frequently utilizing feasible and privately obtained materials. This craftsmanship isn't just a statement of workmanship yet in addition a utilitarian part of Indian homes and insides.

India's house enterprises have forever been firmly connected to the social and financial texture of the country. These businesses have frequently given vocations to underestimated and monetarily distraught networks, offering a method for money and independence. The position framework in India, which generally doled out people to explicit occupations, assumed a part in forming the house business scene. Certain people group represented considerable authority specifically creates, like ceramics, leatherwork, or winding around, and these abilities were passed down from one age to another.

In country regions, the cabin businesses have given a fundamental kind of revenue for some families. The farming based networks frequently take part in cabin ventures during their slow times of year, empowering them to enhance their rural pay. For the overwhelming majority ladies in provincial India, cabin enterprises like handloom winding around and handiworks have offered business potential open doors that permit them to add to their family's pay while telecommuting.

One of the crucial parts of India's cabin ventures is their job in safeguarding social legacy and customs. The development of handloom materials, customary handiworks, and distinctive furniture is in many cases well established in nearby traditions and practices. These specialties act as an unmistakable connection to the past, permitting networks to keep up with their exceptional social personalities and pass down their practices to people in the future.

The bungalow business' association with custom isn't restricted to the actual items yet stretches out to the procedures and abilities utilized in their creation. Craftsmans who practice these artworks are in many cases managers of old information and procedures, guaranteeing that the verifiable underpinnings of these enterprises are safeguarded for any kind of future family. Through apprenticeships and family customs, the abilities are given over starting with one age then onto the next.

Generally speaking, the cabin business plays had an essential impact in advancing and protecting customary fine arts, particularly despite modernization and globalization. For instance, different types of traditional dance and music in India frequently depend on ensembles and instruments made by neighborhood craftsmans. The safeguarding of these works of art, alongside the mind boggling outfits and instruments utilized in exhibitions, is inseparably connected to the bungalow business.

2.2 Influence of ancient textile trade and craftsmanship.

The specialty of material creation is one of the most old and persevering through types of craftsmanship. From the earliest developments to the cutting edge world, materials play had an essential impact in molding economies, societies, and social orders.

The authentic groundworks of material exchange and craftsmanship are well established in mankind's set of experiences, making a permanent imprint on our reality. This account dives into the multifaceted and extensive impact of old material exchange and craftsmanship.

The starting points of material creation can be followed back to the actual sunrise of human civilization. As early agrarian social orders progressed to settled horticultural networks, the requirement for apparel, cover, and different products prompted the advancement of fundamental winding around and sewing strategies. Plant filaments, like flax and cotton, and creature strands, similar to fleece and silk, were among the principal materials used to make materials.

The verifiable underpinnings of material creation can be tracked down in old Egypt, where the Nile Stream gave a ripe climate to the development of flax and the raising of sheep. The material created from flax was one of the earliest material filaments utilized by people. As well as dress, cloth was utilized for sails, bed materials, and stylized articles of clothing. Antiquated Egyptians succeeded in the craft of winding around and were known for their fine material materials.

In India, the historical backdrop of material creation goes back millennia, with cotton being the essential fiber of decision. Cotton plants were developed in the Indus Valley around 2500 BCE, making India one of the earliest focuses of cotton development and cotton-based material creation. The verifiable underpinnings of India's material craftsmanship were established in the development of cotton and the resulting improvement of winding around and coloring methods.

Material craftsmanship in old India was exceptionally refined and impacted by different local customs. The colored and printed cotton materials of India, known as chintz, became popular for their complicated examples and lively varieties. These materials found their direction to far off lands through shipping lanes, making India a central member in the old material exchange organization.

China, one more old center of material creation, contributed essentially to the verifiable underpinnings of material exchange and craftsmanship. The Chinese were gifted weavers and dyers, involving silk as an essential material. The unbelievable Silk Street, an immense organization of shipping lanes that associated East and West, was instrumental in the spread of silk, alongside different products, societies, and thoughts. The Chinese syndication on silk creation for quite a long time assumed an essential part in the worldwide material exchange.

In the Mediterranean locale, the city of Tire, situated in cutting edge Lebanon, was prestigious for its creation of Tyrian purple, a profoundly pursued color extricated from the shells of Murex snails. Tyrian purple was utilized to variety materials, especially for sovereignty and the world class. The color was so costly and work escalated to deliver that it turned into an image of riches and status.

The impact of antiquated material exchange and craftsmanship stretched out past material merchandise; it had extensive social, monetary, and social results. Shipping lanes, for example, the Silk Street and the Incense Course, took into consideration the trading of materials, flavors, valuable metals, and thoughts between various civilizations. The progression of materials among East and West worked with social trades, presenting new plans, themes, and strategies to far off districts.

One of the most momentous parts of the authentic underpinnings of material exchange and craftsmanship is the job of materials as superficial points of interest and social markers. In old Mesopotamia, for instance, fine materials, frequently decorated with perplexing examples and images, were related with social and financial status. The wearing of sumptuous pieces of clothing meant one's situation in the public eye and conveyed a feeling of power.

The equivalent can be seen in antiquated India, where materials held social and profound importance. The holy text, the Rigveda, contains references to the utilization of materials in strict ceremonies and as contributions to gods. Materials were frequently used to make elaborate pieces of clothing for gods, displaying the mind boggling craftsmanship of the time.

In old China, silk was a product as well as an image of riches and eminence. It turned into a vital piece of Chinese culture, and its creation and exchange were exceptionally directed. The Silk Street filled in as a course for social trade, empowering Chinese silk to arrive at far off terrains and impact creative customs, especially in the Mediterranean and Europe.

The verifiable underpinnings of material exchange and craftsmanship are likewise firmly connected to the improvement of early exchange organizations and financial frameworks. In old times, the trading of materials and different wares was in many cases led through deal frameworks, with materials filling in as a type of money. In the Mediterranean, the worth of materials, including colored and woven textures, was a basic part of exchange among districts and societies.

The impact of material exchange stretched out not exclusively to the material and financial parts of society yet additionally to the social and political designs. In old Egypt, for example, the material business was profoundly coordinated, with a division of work in view of orientation. Ladies commonly took part in turning and winding, while men zeroed in on horticulture and the consideration of animals. This division of work had huge ramifications for social elements and orientation jobs.

The spread of material exchange and craftsmanship significantly affected the improvement of domains and developments. The interest for extravagance materials, for example, silk and fine fleece, drove financial development and affected political power structures. The Byzantine Realm, for instance, was known for its silk creation and exchange, which produced significant income and added to the domain's riches and impact.

In India, the Mauryan and Gupta domains (fourth century BCE to the sixth century CE) were instrumental in the turn of events and advancement of materials. These domains supported the development of cotton and the creation of fine materials. The Mauryan ruler Ashoka, specifically, upheld the material business and empowered exchange with locales as far off as Rome. The rich custom of material craftsmanship went on under the Gupta Realm, which was known for its mind boggling silk materials.

The verifiable groundworks of material exchange and craftsmanship assumed a vital part in the improvement of shipping lanes and organizations that crossed landmasses. The Silk Street, which associated China with the Mediterranean, was a demonstration of the persevering through impact of materials on worldwide trade. It worked with the trading of silk as well as different products, thoughts, and societies. The Silk Street advanced social dissemination, prompting the spread of information, innovations, and imaginative impacts.

In the Mediterranean district, the exchange of materials and coloring materials assumed a focal part in the improvement of exchange organizations. Urban areas like Tire, known for their development of Tyrian purple, became vital participants in Mediterranean exchange. The broad shipping lanes that mismatched the Mediterranean associated the people groups of the district and worked with the trading of merchandise and thoughts.

The verifiable underpinnings of material exchange and craftsmanship are firmly entwined with the improvement of developments and the rise of incredible realms. For example, the Byzantine Domain's command over the silk shipping lanes gave it financial and political impact an over a tremendous area. The domain's silk creation was a strictly confidential mystery, and the information was gone down through ages. This imposing business model permitted the Byzantines to extricate recognition from adjoining powers in return for silk.

In old India, the silk exchange significantly affected the economy, and India turned into a huge exporter of silk materials. The exchange of silk with Southeast Asia, the Center East, and the Mediterranean improved the locale and assumed an essential part in the improvement of shipping lanes. Silk materials were sought after, for their flawless quality as well as for the social and social importance related with them.

The impact of old material exchange and craftsmanship reached out to workmanship and feel. The plan and ornamentation of materials, as well as the colors utilized in their creation, have made an enduring imprint on the craftsmanship and culture of various developments. In India, the specialty of block printing, weaving, and coloring created materials with complex plans and examples, mirroring the rich social variety of the subcontinent.

The verifiable groundworks of material exchange and craftsmanship are clear in different creative customs. In old Mesopotamia, chamber seals frequently portrayed scenes of material creation, mirroring the social significance of materials in the public eye. These seals caught the complexities of winding around and turning, giving a visual record of the craftsmanship of the time.

In old India, material plans and themes found their direction into different artistic expressions. The Ajanta and Ellora caves, for instance, are eminent for their mind boggling frescoes that grandstand scenes from Indian life, including portrayals of material creation, clothing, and curtain. The Indian craft of winding around and material plan was additionally displayed in figures and works of art.

In China, the craft of silk winding around and weaving affected customary Chinese workmanship and culture. Complex silk canvases and materials decorated royal residences, sanctuaries, and homes, and the social meaning of silk is apparent in Chinese craftsmanship, writing, and old stories.

The authentic groundworks of material exchange and craftsmanship have made a permanent imprint on the advancement of innovation and development. The interest for materials prompted progressions in turning and winding around methods, as well as coloring.

2.3 Impact of the East India Company and colonial-era industries.

The East India Organization, perhaps of the most persuasive element throughout the entire existence of expansionism, assumed a critical part in forming the financial and political scene of India during the pioneer period. Laid out in 1600, this English exchanging organization started its tasks India in the mid seventeenth 100 years and immediately extended its impact. The effect of the East India Organization, alongside the modern and financial improvements that went with English pioneer rule, had significant ramifications for India's set of experiences, changing it into a province and thusly a central participant in the worldwide economy.

The East India Organization's underlying connections with India were driven in terms of professional career. In the mid seventeenth 100 years, the organization set up general stores along the Indian coast, essentially for the import of products like flavors, materials, and indigo. It was the last option, indigo, which denoted the organization's entrance into India's horticultural and modern scene. Indigo was popular in Europe for coloring materials and was developed in Bengal.

The organization, through different business methodologies, including rent and land income assortment, empowered indigo development among nearby ranchers. In any case, these practices were much of the time shady, prompting agitation and opposition among Indian ranchers. This early experience set the vibe for the East India Organization's association in India's horticulture and businesses.

As the organization extended its command over different districts of India, it utilized its power to propel its financial advantages. The Bengal district, which was a fruitful and thickly populated region, was an especially rewarding concentration. The organization embraced approaches that permitted it to remove income from Indian land and assets. One eminent model was the Super durable Settlement Demonstration of

1793 in Bengal, which presented a proper land income that essentially troubled the neighborhood working class.

This financial double-dealing straightforwardly affected Indian ventures. Land and assets that might have been utilized for farming expansion or the advancement of house businesses were frequently redirected to fulfill the organization's income needs. The provincial organization focused on the development of money crops like indigo, jute, and opium, which were popular in Europe, over food crops or modern harvests that could have helped the Indian economy and modern turn of events.

In the domain of materials, the East India Organization's approaches had sweeping ramifications. India had a rich custom of material creation, including cotton, silk, and fleece, which were exceptionally sought after both locally and in global exchange. The organization started trading Indian materials to England, making rivalry with the home-grown material industry. To safeguard the interests of English makers, the English Parliament passed the Calico Demonstration in 1700 and the later Material Demonstrations, which limited the import of Indian materials into England.

The effect of these guidelines was twofold. From one perspective, it smothered India's material commodities to England, restricting monetary open doors for Indian craftsmans and makers. Then again, it boosted the development of the English material industry, laying the preparation for the Modern Upset. Thus, England started creating materials at a scale and effectiveness that far outperformed India's cabin enterprises, further worsening the financial divergence between the two districts.

The East India Organization's association in India's zest exchange additionally had huge ramifications. The zest exchange was a significant worldwide industry, and the organization looked to overwhelm it. In its quest for command over the zest exchange, the organization utilized both financial and military means to extend its impact in South India and Sri Lanka. This disturbed neighborhood exchange networks as well as achieved clashes and changes in nearby administration structures.

The effect of the organization's activities was not restricted to the monetary circle; it likewise stretched out to the political and social texture of India. The organization's approaches and expansionist exercises frequently brought about political unsteadiness and struggle in various districts. The Clash of Plassey in 1757 and the ensuing control of Bengal denoted a defining moment in the organization's impact in India. The organization laid out its true rule over huge domains, and its confidential armed force, made out of Indian sepoys and European fighters, assumed an essential part in keeping up with control.

The effect of the East India Organization was especially obvious in the improvement of provincial time businesses. English frontier rule and the industrialization of England fundamentally impacted India's financial and modern scene. The Modern Upset, which started in England in the late eighteenth 100 years, altered the creation and assembling processes. With the presentation of automated innovation, steam motors, and new transportation frameworks, England quickly extended its modern result.

The impact of the Modern Upheaval was felt in each part of pilgrim time businesses in India. The most prominent effect was on the material business. The coming of the power loom and turning hardware in England made it conceivable to create materials for an enormous scope, bringing about lower creation costs and expanded productivity. These advances were acquainted with India, principally in the material places of Bombay and Ahmedabad.

The effect on India's bungalow material industry was significant. Handloom weavers, who had been delivering materials for quite a long time utilizing conventional techniques, were out of nowhere confronted with contest from motorized plants. English materials overflowed the Indian market, offering purchasers less expensive and all the more promptly accessible choices. Therefore, India's customary handloom area attempted to contend and confronted a decrease popular.

The impact of English industrialization likewise reached out to other pilgrim time enterprises. The iron and steel industry, for example, was created to fulfill the needs of the growing English railroad framework. India's iron and steel industry turned into a pivotal provider of unrefined components for English rail development, with iron mineral and coal stores being vigorously taken advantage of. The financial interests of the English organization frequently supplanted the advancement of homegrown businesses.

The effect of the pilgrim time enterprises on Indian culture and work was diverse. The motorization of assembling prompted a change in labor elements. Processing plants required a labor force that was unique in relation to the customary work framework, prompting the development of another class of modern workers. The requests of the pioneer time ventures impacted examples of urbanization as individuals moved to urban areas looking for work amazing open doors.

The impact of pilgrim period enterprises on work was not restricted to metropolitan regions. In provincial locales, the requests of money crop development, driven by the East India Organization's income assortment strategies, had huge outcomes. Indian ranchers moved their concentration to cash crops like indigo and opium, redirecting area and work from food crop creation. This shift had repercussions on the food security of the populace and rustic economies.

The effect of the English pioneer organization and the development of pilgrim time businesses should be visible in the advancement of transportation and foundation. The development of rail lines, streets, and transmit lines was driven by English interests and the need to interface different districts for managerial and monetary purposes. While these advancements further developed transportation and correspondence, they were fundamentally designed for working with the commodity of unrefined components and merchandise to England.

The impact of frontier period ventures and the English organization additionally reached out to instruction and culture. Western school systems were presented, and English turned into the mechanism of guidance. The effect of these instructive changes was twofold. On one hand, they gave new open doors to Indians to get to present day training, which at last assumed an essential part in the Indian freedom development. Then again, they planned to create a class of Indian civil servants who might help the English organization.

The impact of pilgrim time businesses and the English organization was not uniform across India. Various locales encountered the effect in an unexpected way, contingent upon variables like topography, financial assets, and pioneer strategies. For instance, regions with important assets like coal, iron, and tea saw expanded interest in framework and industry.

Interestingly, districts with restricted admittance to assets frequently confronted monetary difficulties, as the pilgrim organization zeroed in on removing assets as opposed to advancing neighborhood ventures. The effect on the financial scene of various locales was in this manner set apart by differences and disparities.

The effect of the East India Organization and frontier period businesses on India was critical, changing the country in various ways. The organization's underlying association in exchange laid the foundation for its venture into regional control. The extraction of income, presentation of new yields, and the spread of English industrialization formed India's financial scene.

The effect of the provincial period enterprises, including materials, iron and steel, and transportation, introduced another time of financial turn of events, urbanization, and work elements. Nonetheless, it likewise prompted the downfall of conventional ventures and the reorientation of Indian agribusiness.

The impact of the English organization's strategies stretched out to instruction, language, and culture, leaving an enduring heritage on Indian culture. The effect of English expansionism in India was mind boggling, set apart by the two headways and double-dealing. The verifiable underpinnings of this period keep on forming the present day financial and political scene of the nation, making it fundamental .

3

Chapter 3

The Age of Public Enterprises

The idea of public undertakings, frequently alluded to as state-claimed endeavors (SOEs) or government-possessed companies, has a long history that traces all the way back to old civilizations, however it acquired conspicuousness and developed essentially during the twentieth hundred years. Public ventures are organizations claimed and worked by states at different levels, from the nearby to the public. They cover an expansive scope of ventures, including utilities, transportation, medical care, and assembling. This story investigates the verifiable turn of events, reasoning, difficulties, and effect of the period of public ventures, with an emphasis on the twentieth 100 years.

Authentic Roots and Early Open Undertakings

Public undertakings have profound authentic roots, with instances of state possession and activity of monetary exercises tracing all the way back to antiquated developments. In antiquated Rome, for example, the state controlled different businesses, including mining, public streets, and water supply. In China, state-claimed endeavors assumed a pivotal part in the supreme organization, directing exercises like salt and iron creation.

Be that as it may, the idea of public undertakings as we probably are aware them today started to come to fruition during the nineteenth hundred years, especially following the modern transformation and the advancement of current free enterprise. Because of quick industrialization and urbanization, state run administrations began to mediate in the economy to address social and monetary difficulties. This mediation took different structures, including the foundation of government-possessed undertakings.

One of the earliest and most famous instances of public endeavors was the advancement of the English rail line framework during the nineteenth 100 years. The development and activity of the railroad network were driven by a blend of private and public speculations. The state assumed a huge part in controlling and supervising this basic transportation framework.

Public endeavors likewise assumed a crucial part in the improvement of the American West during the nineteenth 100 years. The central government conceded land and endowments to privately owned businesses to assemble the cross-country railroad, which worked with toward the west development. The progress of this try showed the expected advantages of government association in enormous scope framework projects.

The twentieth Hundred years: The Extension of Public Undertakings

The twentieth century saw a critical development of public ventures around the world. The explanations behind this extension were different and setting explicit, mirroring the interesting monetary, political, and social conditions of every country. Nonetheless, a few normal elements added to the ascent of public endeavors during this period.

Monetary Turn of events and Foundation: As nations industrialized and urbanized, there was a developing requirement for fundamental framework, for example, power, water supply, and transportation organizations. Legislatures perceived the significance of offering these types of assistance to advance monetary turn of events and work on the personal satisfaction for their residents.

Financial Preparation: The experience of The Second Great War and the monetary difficulties of the Economic crisis of the early 20s prompted a reexamination of free enterprise private enterprise. Numerous states embraced monetary preparation and mediation as a way to balance out their economies and relieve the adverse consequences of market instability.

Social Government assistance and Value: Public endeavors were viewed as a method for tending to social disparities and work on expectations for everyday comforts. Areas like medical care, training, and lodging became areas of concentration for state intercession, fully intent on guaranteeing widespread admittance to fundamental administrations.

Public safety: with regards to war and international strains during the twentieth hundred years, legislatures frequently nationalized key ventures, especially those connected with safeguard, to guarantee public safety and independence. State command over energy assets and weighty ventures turned into a typical practice.

Philosophical Movements: The ascent of communist and socialist belief systems in the twentieth century additionally affected the extension of public undertakings. Numerous nations with communist or blended market directions laid out state-possessed undertakings for the purpose of accomplishing aggregate proprietorship and command over key businesses.

The effect of these variables fluctuated by nation and locale. A few countries, especially in Western Europe, embraced blended market economies that consolidated confidential undertaking areas of strength for with mediation. Others, similar to the Soviet Association and its satellite states in Eastern Europe, embraced far reaching state responsibility for method for creation.

Public Endeavors in the Western World

In Western Europe, the mid-twentieth century saw the foundation and development of public ventures in different areas. The reasoning behind these drives frequently incorporated the need to modify and modernize economies after The Second Great War, as well as to give social government assistance and address imbalances. A couple of outstanding models represent the extension and effect of public undertakings in Western Europe:

Nationalization of Key Businesses: In the Unified Realm, the postwar Work government drove by Forebearing Attlee nationalized a few key enterprises, including coal mining, power, gas, and railroads. The objective was to guarantee public control and evenhanded admittance to these fundamental administrations.

Government assistance State and Medical services: In Nordic nations like Sweden, Denmark, and Norway, the improvement of complete government assistance states included government responsibility for areas, like medical care, training, and public transportation. These actions were essential for a more extensive social-vote based plan.

Blended Economy in France: France sought after a blended economy model, with state proprietorship coinciding with private endeavor. The French government kept up with command over key enterprises like aviation, protection, and media communications. This approach meant to figure out some kind of harmony between state intercession and market-driven financial development.

Germany's Public Banks: Germany's Sparkassen (investment funds banks) and Landesbanken (state banks) are instances of fruitful public ventures. These organizations assumed a basic part in neighborhood monetary turn of events, giving admittance to credit and monetary administrations for little and medium-sized ventures (SMEs).

Public Endeavors in the Creating Scene

The development of public endeavors was not restricted to Western industrialized nations. Numerous recently free countries in Asia, Africa, and Latin America likewise settled state-claimed ventures as a component of their endeavors to accomplish financial autonomy and social turn of events. These nations frequently sought after import replacement industrialization (ISI) techniques, where they intended to decrease dependence on imported products by creating homegrown enterprises.

One of the most outstanding instances of this approach was India, which sought after a blended economy model. The Indian government laid out open undertakings in areas like weighty industry, steel, mining, and energy. These undertakings assumed a focal part in the country's financial turn of events and confidence.

In Africa, public endeavors were laid out in areas like agribusiness, mining, transportation, and media communications. These drives were much of the time driven by the longing to tackle regular assets for home-grown turn of events and to lessen reliance on unfamiliar partnerships.

In Latin America, nations like Mexico and Brazil additionally em-braced state proprietorship in different businesses. The nationalization of oil and gas assets was a typical subject, driven by the objective of catching a more prominent portion of the monetary advantages got from these areas.

Difficulties and Reactions

Notwithstanding their aims and accomplishments, public endeavors confronted a few difficulties and reactions during the twentieth 100 years. A portion of the major questions included:

Shortcoming: Public ventures were frequently condemned for be-ing less effective and less receptive to market influences contrasted with private organizations. Administration, absence of rivalry, and political impedance were refered to as elements adding to failure.

Debasement and Blunder: The shortfall of market discipline in a few public undertakings could prompt defilement and botch. Political arrangements and absence of straightforwardness were related with these issues.

Monetary Strain: State possession frequently required critical mon-etary assets. The weight of supporting public endeavors could strain government financial plans, especially in nations with restricted income sources.

Overextend and Syndication: at times, public ventures broadened their exercises past their center capabilities and went into organizations inconsequential to their central goal. This could bring about monopolistic way of behaving and a smothering of rivalry.

Philosophical and Political Pressures: The philosophical and political discussions encompassing public possession prompted strains and clashes. The philosophical battle during the Virus Battle, with its attention on free enterprise versus communism, affected these discussions.

Public Undertakings in the Late twentieth Hundred years and Then some

The late twentieth century saw a change in financial reasoning, with a developing accentuation on market-situated changes, progression, and privatization. A few variables added to this shift:

Monetary Emergencies: Numerous nations confronted financial emergencies, and the failures and monetary weights related with public endeavors went under expanded examination. Accordingly, legislatures tried to rebuild and change state-possessed endeavors.

Changing Philosophical Scene: The breakdown of the Soviet Association and the finish of the Virus War significantly affected the philosophical scene. Market-situated private enterprise turned out to be more predominant, prompting a decrease in the allure of state possession.

Progressions in Monetary Hypothesis: Advances in financial hypothesis, especially in the fields of public decision hypothesis and modern association, shed light on the difficulties and constraints of public proprietorship.

3.1 Examination of the role of public sector giants in post-independence India.

The period following India's freedom in 1947 denoted a critical crossroads in the country's set of experiences, portrayed by a guarantee to financial independence and civil rights. A vital part of India's post-freedom financial technique was the foundation and development of public area ventures, frequently alluded to as open area endeavors (PSUs) or public area units (PSUs). This account dives into the job of these public area goliaths in molding the direction of post-freedom India's economy, society, and advancement.

Verifiable Setting: The Introduction of Public Area Endeavors

The choice to lay out and grow public area endeavors in post-freedom India was well established in the more extensive political, monetary, and social yearnings of the country. It arose as a reaction to the frontier tradition of financial double-dealing, discriminatory abundance circulation, and underdevelopment. India's chiefs, including Jawaharlal Nehru, were directed by a dream of accomplishing monetary independence, decreasing neediness, and limiting financial differences.

The Modern Strategy Goal of 1948 and the resulting Modern Approach of 1956 set the system for the foundation of a blended economy, in which both the confidential area and the public area would coincide and add to the country's turn of events. The public area was imagined as assuming a vital part in essential enterprises, fundamental administrations, and monetary framework. This vision mirrored a pledge to communism and a confidence in the capacity of the state to shape monetary results.

The development of public area ventures was especially articulated in center areas like energy, weighty industry, steel, mining, media communications, and transportation. These areas were considered fundamental for accomplishing independence and advancing industrialization. The foundation of notorious PSUs like BHEL (Bharat Weighty Electricals Restricted), NTPC (Public Nuclear energy Partnership), and SAIL (Steel Authority of India Restricted) flagged the public authority's obligation to indigenization and innovative independence.

Key Goals and Accomplishments

The job of public area goliaths in post-freedom India was complex, enveloping a scope of key goals and accomplishments:

Monetary Independence: Public area endeavors assumed an essential part in decreasing India's reliance on imported products and advancing homegrown industrialization. They were key to the improvement of basic framework, including power plants, steel factories, and media communications organizations.

Work Age: The foundation and extension of public area undertakings contributed essentially to work creation. These ventures utilized an enormous and different labor force, including engineers, specialists, managerial staff, and workers. The effect on business was especially articulated in locales with a weighty centralization of PSUs.

Innovation Move and Development: Public area monsters worked with the exchange of innovation and information to India. A considerable lot of them went into joint efforts and organizations with unfamiliar organizations, prompting the obtaining of cutting edge innovation and mastery. This information trade added to India's specialized capacities and innovative work endeavors.

Value and Civil rights: Public area endeavors were viewed as instruments of advancing civil rights and lessening financial disparities. They assumed a basic part in conveying fundamental administrations like medical services, schooling, and transportation to the majority. This obligation to public government assistance lined up with the standards of popularity based communism.

Adjusting the Confidential Area: Public area endeavors were intended to coincide with the confidential area, giving an offset to the grouping of monetary power in confidential hands. This was seen as a method for guaranteeing that the advantages of financial development were all the more fairly disseminated.

Territorial Turn of events: The area of public area ventures frequently impacted local turn of events. Modern municipalities and bunches conformed to these ventures, prompting urbanization, further developed framework, and the rise of nearby organizations and administrations.

Public Area Monsters and the Indian Economy

Public area endeavors assumed a critical part in forming India's economy during the post-freedom time frame. Their commitments were clear in a few key areas:

Energy and Power Age: Public area endeavors like NTPC and NHPC (Public Hydroelectric Power Partnership) assumed a critical part in India's power age and dispersion. These goliaths were instrumental in tending to India's constant power deficiencies and growing the country's power network.

Steel and Weighty Industry: PSUs in the steel and weighty industry areas, including SAIL and BHEL, supported the country's modern base and added to its independence in key materials. These monsters helped in the creation of steel, hardware, and weighty gear required for framework improvement.

Mining and Normal Assets: Ventures like Coal India Restricted and ONGC (Oil and Flammable gas Enterprise) were indispensable for bridling India's regular assets, guaranteeing a predictable stock of coal, oil, and gas for modern use and energy creation.

Broadcast communications: BSNL (Bharat Sanchar Nigam Restricted) and MTNL (Mahanagar Phone Nigam Restricted) were instrumental in growing India's media communications framework and giving reasonable admittance to telecom administrations, particularly in rustic regions.

Aviation and Protection: The foundation of PSUs like HAL (Hindustan Air transportation Restricted) and DRDO (Safeguard Innovative work Association) assumed a significant part in creating native guard capacities and aviation advances.

Difficulties and Reactions

While public area monsters made huge commitments to India's post-freedom advancement, they likewise confronted various difficulties and reactions. A portion of the main points of contention included:

Administration and Shortcoming: Public area undertakings were frequently reprimanded for regulatory failures, absence of development, and slow dynamic cycles. The shortfall of market discipline could prompt carelessness and failure.

Political Impedance: The impact of political contemplations on the working of PSUs could result in less than ideal direction. Arrangements, advancements, and strategy choices were now and then affected by political interests.

Absence of Independence: PSUs frequently worked under an administrative system that compelled their independence and seriousness. They confronted limitations on valuing, venture, and extension, which could thwart their presentation.

Monetary Weight: Numerous public area goliaths confronted monetary difficulties, with some of them amassing critical obligation. Their reliance on government subsidizing and appropriations could strain government funds.

Rivalry from the Confidential Area: Public area ventures confronted expanding contest from the confidential area, particularly as India changed its economy during the 1990s. Some PSUs attempted to adjust to the changing industry climate and market elements.

Mechanical Out of date quality: The accentuation on state possession some of the time prompted an absence of motivations for innovative development. Some PSUs confronted difficulties in staying up with worldwide mechanical progressions.

Financial Changes and Advancement

The late twentieth century saw a huge change in India's financial strategy, described by monetary changes and progression. The milestone financial changes of 1991, frequently alluded to as the New Monetary Strategy, denoted a defining moment in India's monetary direction. These changes tried to address the difficulties and reactions related with public area undertakings while embracing market-arranged approaches.

Key components of the monetary changes included:

Progression: The destroying of the Permit Raj, an arrangement of regulatory licenses and guidelines that confined financial exercises, considered more noteworthy market section and contest.

Privatization: The public authority started the course of privatization, which included the offer of state-possessed undertakings to private financial backers. This was finished fully intent on decreasing the public authority's monetary weight and further developing proficiency.

Globalization: India progressively incorporated into the worldwide economy, opening up to unfamiliar ventures and exchange. The progression of exchange and speculation strategies empowered unfamiliar direct venture (FDI) and added to financial development.

Rebuilding and Disinvestment: The public authority left on a course of rebuilding and disinvestment in open area endeavors. This included stripping halfway possession and permitting more prominent independence to PSUs.

The Effect on Open Area Monsters

The monetary changes and progression altogether affected public area monsters in India. While a portion of the bigger and more proficient PSUs kept on flourishing, others confronted more noteworthy difficulties. The effect on PSUs fluctuated relying upon the area and the endeavor's versatility and productivity.

Proficiency and Development: The changes boosted public area ventures to turn out to be more productive and creative. Some PSUs adjusted to the changing climate by embracing innovation, smoothing out activities, and improving their seriousness.

Rivalry: Expanded contest from the confidential area constrained PSUs to work on their exhibition and administrations. In areas like media communications, this opposition prompted more noteworthy effectiveness and administration quality.

Key Disinvestment: The public authority's approach of vital disinvestment brought about the offer of offers in a few public area undertakings to private financial backers. This permitted the public authority to raise reserves and diminish its monetary weight.

3.2 key public enterprises such as SAIL, BHEL, and IOC.

Public area ventures play had a critical impact in molding the monetary and modern scene of India since its freedom in 1947. Among the huge number of public area endeavors (PSUs), three key monsters that considerably affect the country's advancement are Steel Authority of India Restricted (SAIL), Bharat Weighty Electricals Restricted (BHEL), and Indian Oil Partnership (IOC). This story looks at the beginnings, advancement, and commitments of these public endeavors to India's development and improvement.

Steel Authority of India Restricted (SAIL): Fashioning India's Modern Spine

Laid out in 1973, the Steel Authority of India Restricted (SAIL) is one of the biggest steel-production organizations on the planet. It was framed through the blend of different state-possessed steel organizations and assumed a critical part in changing India into an independent steel maker.

Verifiable Foundation:

SAIL's set of experiences is interlaced with India's quest for financial confidence and industrialization. In the early post-freedom time frame, India was vigorously dependent on steel imports to satisfy its homegrown need. Perceiving the essential significance of the steel business for monetary development and safeguard needs, the Indian government chose to put resources into fostering a vigorous and independent steel area.

Key Achievements:

SAIL has accomplished a few critical achievements in its excursion:

Nationalization of Steel Industry: The nationalization of the steel business during the 1970s made ready for the development of SAIL, merging a few steel plants under a solitary umbrella.

Modernization and Extension: SAIL set out on a monstrous modernization and development program to update its offices and lift creation limit. The organization put resources into new advances, like the reception of the Essential Oxygen Heater (BOF) process, which worked on the quality and effectiveness of steel creation.

Enhancement: SAIL extended past its center steel business into related areas like mining, refractories, and designing consultancy administrations.

Worldwide Presence: SAIL laid out a worldwide impression by sending out its steel items to more than 70 nations and going into joint endeavors and coordinated efforts with global steel monsters.

Social Obligation: SAIL has been effectively engaged with local area advancement, instruction, medical services, and ecological supportability, showing its obligation to corporate social obligation.

Commitments and Effect:

SAIL's commitments to India's improvement are multi-layered:

Confidence in Steel: SAIL's endeavors have altogether decreased India's reliance on steel imports. It plays had a critical impact in satisfying homegrown interest, supporting framework tasks, and meeting the necessities of vital areas like protection.

Business Age: The organization utilizes an immense labor force, including designers, specialists, and workers, adding to work creation and monetary development in locales encompassing its steel plants.

Mechanical Progression: SAIL has reliably put resources into innovation and advancement, which has improved steel quality as well as added to India's specialized abilities and innovative work endeavors.

Territorial Turn of events: SAIL's presence in different pieces of India has prompted local turn of events, including the development of modern municipalities and bunches around its offices.

Natural Drives: The organization has attempted various ecological drives, including afforestation, squander the executives, and water preservation, to limit its natural impression.

Notwithstanding, SAIL has confronted difficulties, including issues connected with shortcoming, overstaffing, and the requirement for proceeded with modernization and variation to showcase elements. The organization's process mirrors India's mission for confidence in basic businesses and its continuous obligation to the development and improvement of the country.

Bharat Weighty Electricals Restricted (BHEL): Driving India's Advancement

Bharat Weighty Electricals Restricted (BHEL) is one of India's biggest designing and assembling ventures, spend significant time in the development of force age gear, modern apparatus, and electrical items. Established in 1964, BHEL plays had a urgent impact in the nation's industrialization and jolt.

Authentic Foundation:

BHEL's foundation was in light of India's developing energy needs and the need for independence in power gear fabricating. At that point, India was intensely reliant upon imports for its power age hardware, making the country defenseless against outside impacts.

Key Achievements:

BHEL has accomplished a few key achievements:

Establishment and Development: BHEL was made by blending a few existing state-possessed substances in the power area. The organization was entrusted with planning, producing, and keeping an extensive variety of force gear.

Innovation Move: BHEL went into joint efforts with driving worldwide makers to procure innovation for the creation of force age hardware. It effectively adjusted and indigenized these innovations.

Enhancement: BHEL differentiated its item reach to incorporate modern hardware, transportation gear, and electrical parts. It additionally ventured into different areas like sustainable power and transportation.

Worldwide Extension: The organization's power hardware tracked down global business sectors in nations across Asia, Africa, and the Center East. BHEL laid out a presence in these districts by providing power plants and gear.

Innovative work: BHEL's obligation to innovative work has prompted advancements in power age innovation and the improvement of cleaner and more effective gear.

Commitments and Effect:

BHEL's commitments to India's advancement are significant:

Energy Framework: BHEL has been instrumental in the improvement of India's energy foundation, giving power age gear and administrations for warm, hydro, atomic, and environmentally friendly power projects.

Work and Expertise Improvement: The organization has been a huge wellspring of business, straightforwardly and in a roundabout way, through its broad production network. BHEL's preparation and expertise advancement drives have added to India's designing and specialized labor force.

Energy Proficiency and Natural Obligation: BHEL's attention on innovative work has brought about the development of additional energy-proficient and harmless to the ecosystem gear. It upholds the country's objectives of lessening fossil fuel byproducts and changing to cleaner energy sources.

Social Drives: The organization has been associated with a few social drives, including medical care, training, and local area improvement, helping the districts around its offices.

Challenges looked by BHEL incorporate rivalry from the confidential area, failures underway, and the requirement for proceeded with modernization to stay aware of mechanical progressions and market requests. The organization's process reflects India's mission for energy independence and its obligation to accomplishing widespread admittance to power.

Indian Oil Partnership (IOC): Filling India's Versatility and Development

The Indian Oil Enterprise (IOC) is one of the biggest oil and gas organizations in India and the world. Laid out in 1959, IOC assumes a basic part in guaranteeing the energy security of the country by refining, dispersing, and showcasing oil based commodities.

Verifiable Foundation:

IOC's development was a reaction to the requirement for energy security and the administration of India's oil and gas assets. Before its foundation, the oil and gas area in India was prevalently under unfamiliar control, making the country helpless against outside impacts.

Key Achievements:

IOC has accomplished a few huge achievements in its excursion:

Nationalization and Extension: The public authority of India nationalized the oil business in 1976, prompting the making of a solitary, coordinated substance, the Indian Oil Organization. The organization extended its refining limit, pipeline organization, and circulation framework.

Enhancement: IOC differentiated its tasks into different fragments, including petrochemicals, investigation and creation, and environmentally friendly power sources.

Retail Extension: The organization laid out a huge organization of retail outlets, offering oil based commodities and administrations across the length and expansiveness of India. The compass of its retail network has made oil based commodities available to the majority.

Energy Effectiveness and Ecological Obligation: IOC has zeroed in on improving energy proficiency and diminishing natural effects. It has likewise wandered into cleaner and sustainable power sources.

Examination and Advancement: The organization has put resources into exploration and development to foster cleaner energizes and oils and work on the presentation and productivity of its items.

Commitments and Effect:

IOC's commitments to India's improvement are colossal:

Energy Security: The organization assumes a urgent part in guaranteeing a steady stockpile of oil based commodities to fulfill the energy needs of the country. It has added to diminishing India's reliance on oil imports.

Work Creation: IOC is perhaps of the biggest business in India, giving immediate and backhanded work open doors across different fragments of its tasks.

Versatility and Access: The broad retail organization of IOC guarantees that oil based goods are promptly open to the populace, supporting transportation, industry, and farming.

Ecological Obligation: IOC has been effectively associated with drives to lessen its carbon impression, foster cleaner fills, and advance natural maintainability.

Social Drives: The organization has embraced social drives, including medical care, training, and local area improvement, helping the districts around its offices.

3.3 Contributions to infrastructure development and economic growth.

Framework improvement assumes a significant part in the financial development and in general advancement of a country. It envelops the development and upkeep of basic frameworks, for example, transportation, energy, water supply, and media communications, which structure the foundation of an economy. This account investigates the key meaning of framework improvement in driving financial development, drawing from worldwide and provincial guides to feature commitments and the difficulties accompany it.

The Foundation of Financial Development

Framework improvement is frequently alluded to as the foundation of financial development for a few convincing reasons:

Assistance of Exchange and Business: Present day transportation framework, including streets, rail routes, ports, and air terminals, is essential for the proficient development of labor and products. It decreases transportation costs, upgrades market access, and cultivates exchange and business, adding to monetary development.

Energy Creation and Appropriation: Dependable and available energy foundation is principal for modern cycles, business exercises, and families. It supports monetary development by fueling plants, workplaces, homes, and mechanical headways.

Human Resources and Training: Foundation improvement as instructive organizations, like schools and colleges, is instrumental in making a gifted labor force. A knowledgeable and gifted labor force, thusly, advances financial development and advancement.

Medical services Offices: Open medical care framework, including medical clinics, facilities, and clinical examination places, assumes a vital part in keeping a useful labor force. It adds to generally prosperity, diminishes mortality, and lifts monetary development.

Media communications and Network: Computerized framework is vital for associating individuals and organizations in the cutting edge time. It empowers remote work, online business, data trade, and the conveyance of administrations, which are all vital to monetary development.

Water Supply and Sterilization: Admittance to perfect and safe water, as well as disinfection offices, is fundamental for general well-being and prosperity. Satisfactory water foundation forestalls sicknesses, further develops efficiency, and supports by and large monetary development.

Worldwide Instances of Framework Driven Development

A few nations and districts have shown the groundbreaking force of framework improvement in energizing financial development. The following are a couple of illustrative models:

1. **China's Framework Blast:** China's fast monetary climb is frequently ascribed to its huge foundation speculations. The nation has constructed a tremendous organization of roadways, fast rail, ports, and air terminals, improving network and supporting its product situated assembling area. This broad foundation improvement has been a critical driver of China's momentous monetary development throughout the course of recent many years.

2. **The US and the Interstate Roadway Framework:** The development of the U.S. Interstate Roadway Framework during the twentieth century extraordinarily worked with the development of individuals and merchandise the nation over. It empowered urbanization, upheld the development of rural networks, and

reinforced financial movement by decreasing transportation expenses and time.

3. **Dubai's Financial Change:** Dubai, a piece of the Unified Bedouin Emirates, has gone through a wonderful change through framework improvement. The city-state put resources into making elite air terminals, seaports, and transportation organizations. This improvement filled its progress from an exchanging center to a worldwide monetary and business focus.

4. **India's Aggressive Foundation Activities:** India's framework advancement drives have been vital to the country's monetary development. The development of the Brilliant Quadrilateral, an organization of four-path thruways interfacing significant urban communities, has essentially decreased transportation costs and improved network. Aggressive tasks like the Delhi Metro, devoted cargo passageways, and environmentally friendly power drives have added to India's fast monetary development.

5. **European Association's Attachment Strategy:** The European Association (EU) has sought after a framework driven union approach that intends to decrease financial inconsistencies among its part states. Interests in transportation, energy, and broadband framework in less-created districts have animated monetary development and combination across the EU.

Difficulties and Bottlenecks

While framework advancement is fundamental for financial development, it accompanies its own arrangement of difficulties and bottlenecks:

Subsidizing and Funding: The sheer expense of framework improvement can be a huge obstacle. Getting satisfactory financing for huge scope tasks can strain government spending plans, prompting monetary difficulties. Creative supporting systems and public-private associations (PPPs) have been utilized to resolve this issue.

Administrative Obstacles: Administrative deterrents, including complex allowing processes and regulatory formality, can block the convenient execution of foundation projects. Smoothing out guidelines and working on the simplicity of carrying on with work are fundamental for assisting advancement.

Support and Maintainability: Ignoring the support and upkeep of existing foundation can prompt its corruption and shortcoming. Guaranteeing the maintainability of foundation resources, especially even with natural difficulties, is a basic thought.

Natural and Social Effect: Foundation advancement can have unfriendly ecological and social results while possibly not painstakingly arranged and executed. Offsetting monetary development with natural maintainability and social prosperity is a complicated test.

Framework Holes: Variations in foundation access among metropolitan and provincial regions or among various locales inside a nation can obstruct impartial monetary development. Addressing these holes is crucial to guarantee comprehensive turn of events.

The Job of Innovation in Foundation Improvement

Innovation is progressively assuming a critical part in tending to a large number of the difficulties related with foundation improvement. A few mechanical developments are forming the eventual fate of foundation:

Computerized Framework: The development of advanced foundation, including 5G organizations and rapid web access, is empowering remote work, web based business, and the effective trade of data and administrations.

Brilliant Urban areas: The idea of shrewd urban areas includes the coordination of innovation into metropolitan framework to upgrade proficiency, supportability, and personal satisfaction. It incorporates developments like wise transportation frameworks, squander the board, and energy protection.

Sustainable power: Advances in environmentally friendly power advancements, for example, sun oriented and wind power, are changing the energy framework by giving perfect and feasible other options.

Blockchain and Advanced Twins: Blockchain innovation and computerized twins, which make advanced copies of actual framework, are further developing straightforwardness, recognizability, and the administration of resources.

Framework Checking and Support: The utilization of sensors, drones, and man-made reasoning in foundation observing and upkeep is further developing resource the board and lessening costs.

Natural Alleviation: Innovation is helping address natural difficulties related with foundation improvement through developments like green framework and eco-accommodating materials.

Interest from now on

Putting resources into framework improvement is an interest from now on, and states, global associations, and the confidential area assume basic parts in getting it going. Public-private organizations (PPPs) have acquired unmistakable quality for of drawing in confidential speculation and skill while guaranteeing that foundation projects serve public interests.

The Unified Countries' Reasonable Improvement Objectives (SDGs) incorporate a few targets connected with foundation improvement, underlining the significance of guaranteeing admittance to quality framework while limiting the ecological and social effects. Accomplishing these objectives requires a cooperative exertion between legislatures, the confidential area, and common society.

An Impetus for Thriving

Framework improvement is an impetus for success, empowering financial development, diminishing destitution, and upgrading the personal satisfaction. Whether through the development of transportation organizations, energy age, or advanced availability, framework projects are instrumental in forming the financial directions of countries. The difficulties are critical, yet with creative supporting models, innovative headways, and a guarantee to manageability, the way to evenhanded and reasonable improvement through framework stays open. In a universe of dynamic change and developing necessities, foundation improvement will keep on being a foundation of progress and thriving for social orders all over the planet.

Chapter 4

The IT Revolution

The IT upheaval, which has unfurled throughout the course of recent many years, permanently affects virtually every feature of our lives. It has changed the manner in which we work, convey, access data, and lead business. From the expansion of PCs during the 1980s to the coming of the web and the ascent of cell phones in the 21st hundred years, the IT transformation has been a main impetus of progress and development.

One of the critical parts of the IT insurgency has been the quick progression of equipment and programming advances. In the beginning of figuring, PCs were enormous, costly, and generally restricted to government and scholarly foundations. Notwithstanding, as innovation advanced, PCs decreased, more reasonable, and available to the overall population. The improvement of microchips, which could perform complex estimations in a little chip, upset the business, making it conceivable to make PCs that could fit on a work area or even in a pocket.

In lined up with equipment improvement, programming plays had a basic impact in the IT transformation. Working frameworks like

Microsoft Windows and Apple's Macintosh operating system have become pervasive, giving easy to understand interfaces and empowering a large number of uses. Programming improvement has turned into a roaring industry, with a great many software engineers and designers overall making everything from computer games to efficiency devices. The development of open-source programming, which is unreservedly accessible and cooperatively created, has likewise been a significant driver of development.

The web, a central component of the IT upset, has reshaped the manner in which we access data and convey. In the mid 1990s, the Internet arose, considering the making of sites and simple route through hyperlinks. The web immediately turned into a worldwide organization that associated individuals and data across the world. Email, online talk, and web-based entertainment stages have become fundamental apparatuses for correspondence and social collaboration, empowering individuals to interface with others paying little mind to actual distance.

Online business has likewise been a significant result of the IT unrest. Online commercial centers like Amazon and eBay have changed the manner in which we shop, offering a huge swath of items and administrations that can be bought from the solace of our homes. Advanced installment frameworks, for example, PayPal and digital currencies like Bitcoin, have additionally worked with online exchanges. This shift to web based business has had broad ramifications for customary physical retail organizations and production network the board.

The IT unrest has fundamentally affected the working environment, adjusting the manner in which we work and direct business. The appearance of PCs and office programming like Microsoft Office has smoothed out authoritative undertakings, making it more straightforward to make reports, oversee information, and speak with partners. Joint effort devices, for example, video conferencing and cloud-based project the board stages, have empowered remote work and worldwide business organizations.

Distributed computing has been one more extraordinary part of the IT upset. It permits organizations and people to get to figuring assets, like capacity and handling power, through the web. This has prompted the ascent of programming as a help (SaaS) stages, where clients can get to applications and administrations without the requirement for neighborhood establishments. Distributed computing has additionally been instrumental in information capacity and examination, cultivating the development of enormous information and investigation.

The IT insurgency has reshaped businesses and made new ones. Media outlets, for instance, has seen a total change. Web-based features like Netflix, Hulu, and YouTube have upset conventional TV and film dissemination models. Music streaming stages like Spotify and Apple Music have changed how we consume music. The gaming business has developed from console-based gaming to versatile gaming and online multiplayer encounters. Computer generated reality and expanded reality advances have opened up additional opportunities for vivid diversion.

In medical services, IT significantly affects patient consideration and clinical exploration. Electronic wellbeing records (EHRs) have supplanted paper-based records, making it simpler for medical care suppliers to access and share patient data. Telemedicine has filled in ubiquity, permitting patients to remotely talk with medical services experts. Clinical examination has profited from cutting edge imaging advances, information examination, and man-made consciousness, prompting forward leaps in diagnostics and treatment.

Instruction has likewise been impacted by the IT insurgency. Internet learning stages, as Coursera and edX, offer many courses and degree programs, making training more open to individuals around the world. Learning the board frameworks (LMS) have become vital for schools and colleges, working with the administration of courses, tasks, and appraisals. Computerized course books and open instructive assets have diminished the expense of instructive materials.

The IT upheaval has achieved huge changes in the manner we access news and data. Conventional print papers and magazines have confronted difficulties as perusers progressively go to online news sources and web-based entertainment. Resident reporting and client created content have become necessary to the news scene. Web indexes like Google have made it simpler to track down data, while calculations and customized proposals shape the substance we consume.

Virtual entertainment plays had a noticeable impact in the IT unrest, modifying how we interface with others and communicate our thoughts. Stages like Facebook, Twitter, Instagram, and TikTok have made new types of correspondence and social collaboration. They have likewise been instrumental in forming general assessment, impacting political developments, and spreading data (and falsehood) at a fast speed.

Network safety has turned into a basic worry in the IT transformation. With the expanded dependence on computerized innovation, the gamble of cyberattacks and information breaks has developed. States, associations, and people have needed to put resources into safety efforts to safeguard delicate data. The field of network safety has extended, with experts attempting to protect against dangers and foster secure frameworks.

The IT unrest has changed our regular routines as well as had extensive impacts on society and the economy. It has set out new financial open doors, with the innovation area turning into a significant driver of occupation development and development. Tech new businesses have prospered, drawing in speculation and cultivating enterprising soul. The worldwide tech goliaths, like Apple, Google, Amazon, and Facebook, have turned into a portion of the world's most persuasive and productive organizations.

Be that as it may, the IT transformation has additionally raised issues connected with financial imbalance. The computerized partition, the hole between the people who approach innovation and the web and the people who don't, has enlarged in certain districts and socioeconomics.

While some have received the rewards of the computerized economy, others have been abandoned, battling to get to fundamental administrations and open doors.

The IT unrest has additionally introduced moral and protection concerns. The assortment and investigation of huge measures of individual information have brought up issues about individual protection and information security. The utilization of calculations in dynamic cycles, from employing to loaning, has raised worries about predisposition and separation.

Legislatures and administrative bodies have needed to wrestle with how to safeguard residents' privileges and guarantee that innovation is utilized capably.

Additionally, the IT upset has started banters about the effect of computerization and man-made brainpower hands on market. While these advances can possibly build proficiency and efficiency, they additionally have the ability to mechanize specific undertakings, possibly prompting position dislodging in specific businesses. The fate of work is being reconsidered, with conversations about reskilling and upskilling the labor force to adjust to the advancing position scene.

The ecological effect of the IT transformation is another critical concern. The creation of electronic gadgets and the energy utilization of server farms add to electronic waste and ozone depleting substance emanations. Endeavors are being made to foster more energy-effective innovations and lessen the natural impression of the IT business.

The IT upset has not just changed the manner in which we live and work however has likewise reshaped the manner in which state run administrations work. E-government drives have intended to make taxpayer supported organizations more open and productive through advanced channels. Web based casting a ballot, open information drives, and computerized personality frameworks have been executed to upgrade metro support and government straightforwardness.

The IT insurgency has even stretched out to the domain of room investigation. The utilization of cutting edge PC frameworks and mechanical technology has empowered the investigation of far off planets and the investigation of heavenly bodies. Innovations like the Mars wanderers and the Hubble Space Telescope have given important experiences into the universe.

In the domain of transportation, the IT upheaval has prompted the improvement of independent vehicles. Self-driving vehicles and trucks can possibly alter transportation frameworks, making them more secure and more effective. The combination of man-made intelligence and sensors in vehicles permits them to explore and go with choices freely, opening up additional opportunities for versatility.

The fate of the IT upheaval holds much more commitment and difficulties. Quantum processing, a quickly propelling field, can possibly take care of perplexing issues at speeds impossible with old style PCs. This could have critical ramifications for fields like cryptography, materials science, and medication revelation.

4.1 Exploration of the IT industry's emergence in India.

The rise of the IT business in India has been an exceptional and extraordinary excursion that has fundamentally affected the nation's economy, worldwide innovation scene, and labor force. This investigation digs into the beginnings, development, and effect of the Indian IT industry, revealing insight into the variables that pushed it to the cutting edge of the worldwide innovation area.

In the late twentieth 100 years, India's IT industry was essentially non-existent. The country had recently acquired autonomy from English frontier rule in 1947 and was wrestling with monetary difficulties. In any case, in the mid 1960s and 1970s, India established the groundwork for its IT process with the foundation of instructive and research organizations, like the Indian Foundations of Innovation (IITs) and the Indian Organizations of The board (IIMs). These establishments created a pool of exceptionally talented designers and chiefs who might later assume essential parts in the development of the IT business.

The IT upheaval in India really started in the last part of the 1980s and mid 1990s when the public authority presented monetary changes that changed the Indian economy. Before these changes, India worked in an exceptionally directed and protectionist financial climate, which prevented development and advancement. The progression measures, frequently alluded to as "financial advancement" or "monetary changes," intended to open up the Indian economy to unfamiliar speculation, exchange, and innovation.

One of the critical components of these changes was the unwinding of guidelines that had recently limited unfamiliar direct venture (FDI) in India. This change permitted unfamiliar innovation organizations to lay out a presence in the country, which would demonstrate instrumental in the development of the IT business. The progression of exchange and the decrease of import taxes additionally worked with admittance to innovation and assets.

Simultaneously, the Y2K issue, otherwise called the "Thousand years Bug," was approaching as a worldwide concern. Numerous PC frameworks overall were modified to store dates utilizing just the last two digits of the year, which represented a likely issue as the year 2000 drew nearer. This provoked an unexpected interest for programming experts who could recognize and redress the Y2K issue. India quickly jumping all over this chance and demonstrated its capacities in tending to the Y2K bug, prompting global acknowledgment of its IT ability pool.

All the while, the telecom area in India was going through a change. The liberation of the broadcast communications industry and the presentation of portable communication took into consideration the fast extension of media communications foundation. Further developed availability and the spread of the web became fundamental elements for the development of the IT business.

One of the vital minutes in the rise of the Indian IT industry was the foundation of the Product Innovation Parks of India (STPI) in 1991. STPIs were established to give a helpful climate to IT and programming trades. They offered charge motivating forces, a dependable innovation foundation, and an administrative system that supported unfamiliar interest in the IT area.

The early examples of overcoming adversity of Indian IT organizations like Infosys, Goodbye Consultancy Administrations (TCS), and Wipro started to draw in global consideration.

These organizations gave programming administrations to clients around the world, showing India's capacities in programming advancement, support, and re-appropriating. This obvious the start of India's excursion as a worldwide IT rethinking center point.

One of the characterizing factors that added to the ascent of the Indian IT industry was the accessibility of an exceptionally gifted, English-talking labor force. India's schooling system, which zeroed in on math and science, created an enormous pool of designers and software engineering graduates who were in fact capable as well as capable in English. This capability in English language abilities demonstrated important in the worldwide innovation market, as it worked with successful correspondence with clients and accomplices around the world.

The idea of "offshoring" likewise assumed a huge part in the development of the Indian IT industry. Offshoring includes re-appropriating business cycles or administrations to an area beyond the organization's nation of origin. India arose as a prime offshoring objective because of its expense viability and talented workforce. Organizations in the US and other created nations saw the potential for significant expense reserve funds by reevaluating IT and business cycles to India.

During the 1990s and 2000s, Indian IT organizations fabricated a standing for giving great IT administrations for a portion of the expense of their Western partners. The "worldwide conveyance model" turned into a vital methodology for Indian IT firms. This model included a blend of on location counseling and seaward turn of events, where work was finished in India and conveyed to clients abroad.

One more huge part of the Indian IT industry's development was its enhancement into different areas, including programming improvement, IT administrations, business process re-appropriating (BPO), information process rethinking (KPO), and innovative work. The area took special care of an expansive range of businesses, including finance, medical services, retail, broadcast communications, and that's only the tip of the iceberg.

Indian IT organizations quickly extended their worldwide impression by setting up workplaces and advancement focuses in various nations. This worldwide presence permitted them to serve clients all the more actually and be nearer to their objective business sectors. They laid out serious areas of strength for an in significant innovation center points, including the US, Europe, and Asia.

The Indian government kept on supporting the IT business' development by carrying out strategies that energized business, advancement, and unfamiliar speculation. Unique monetary zones (SEZs) were laid out to give tax breaks and framework backing to IT organizations. The Service of Gadgets and Data Innovation (MeitY) planned approaches to advance innovative work and encourage development in the IT area.

The Indian IT industry likewise profited from its capacity to adjust to new innovations and patterns. As the innovation scene advanced, Indian organizations extended their abilities to include arising fields, for example, portable application improvement, distributed computing, enormous information investigation, and computerized reasoning (man-made intelligence). These organizations put resources into innovative work to remain at the front line of innovation.

The Indian IT industry's development has not been without challenges. One of the constant issues has been the requirement for framework improvement, including solid power and transportation frameworks. Notwithstanding these difficulties, Indian IT organizations have succeeded in conveying IT administrations and answers for a worldwide customers.

The Indian IT industry's part in driving development and computerized change for worldwide organizations couldn't possibly be more significant. Indian IT experts have been associated with spearheading work, including the advancement of programming, calculations, and stages that have altered ventures around the world. The business' commitment to the improvement of worldwide inventory chains, on-line business, fintech, and medical care innovations is obvious.

The effect of the Indian IT industry isn't restricted to the innovation area alone. It plays had a critical impact in making position and supporting the Indian economy. The business has been a critical supporter of India's Gross domestic product and has set out work open doors for a large number of designers, programming engineers, project supervisors, and care staff.

Moreover, the Indian IT industry has been instrumental in ladies' strengthening. Numerous ladies in India have sought after vocations in IT, separating conventional orientation boundaries and adding to their families' monetary prosperity. The business' attention on meritocracy and abilities has given open doors to ladies to succeed in the work environment.

The Indian IT industry's development has likewise been an impetus for the development of other related areas, like land, cordiality, and transportation. As IT centers and innovation parks were laid out in urban areas like Bangalore, Hyderabad, and Pune, these regions saw fast urbanization and financial turn of events.

Nonetheless, the Indian IT industry has not been safe to worldwide financial variances and changes in the business scene. The business confronted difficulties during the worldwide monetary emergency of 2008 and resulting financial slumps. Moreover, the advancement of computerization and simulated intelligence has raised worries about potential work removal, provoking Indian IT organizations to put resources into upskilling and reskilling their labor force.

As of late, there has been a shift towards computerized change, distributed computing, and simulated intelligence driven arrangements. Indian IT firms have embraced these patterns, offering administrations that help clients in their advanced excursion. The business has perceived the need to advance from customary IT administrations to offering higher-benefit administrations like computerized counseling, network protection, and information examination.

The Indian government has kept on supporting the IT business through drives like "Computerized India," which expects to change the country into a carefully engaged society and information economy. These drives center around working on computerized framework, advancing computerized proficiency, and working with e-administration.

Regardless of the huge outcome of the Indian IT industry, it faces continuous difficulties and open doors. The requirement for development and remaining serious in a quickly advancing worldwide scene stays fundamental. Besides, the business should address network safety concerns, information insurance, and administrative consistence as it handles touchy data for clients around the world.

The rise of more up to date advancements like blockchain, quantum registering, and 5G presents new roads for the Indian IT industry to investigate. It is one more to Embrace supportability and ecological obligation.

4.2 Profiles of IT giants like TCS, Infosys, and Wipro.

Goodbye Consultancy Administrations (TCS), Infosys, and Wipro are three of the most unmistakable IT goliaths in India, all in all alluded to as the "Large Three" of the Indian IT industry. These organizations play played urgent parts in molding the worldwide innovation scene, giving an extensive variety of IT administrations and answers for clients across the world. Every one of these goliaths has a special profile, with particular chronicles, plans of action, and commitments to the IT business.

Goodbye Consultancy Administrations (TCS):

TCS, an auxiliary of the Goodbye Gathering, is one of the most seasoned and biggest IT administrations organizations in India. Established in 1968, it was laid out as a division of Goodbye Children, the holding organization of the Goodbye Gathering, to give PC administrations to other Goodbye organizations. TCS's process started when it was entrusted with fostering a native PC, the Goodbye Burroughs 2200, to address the innovation needs of the gathering.

In the early years, TCS principally served the Goodbye Gathering's inward IT needs. In any case, in 1974, it made a huge stride by marking its most memorable client, the National Bank of India, denoting the organization's entrance into the IT administrations industry. This noticeable the start of TCS's progress from an in-house IT division to a worldwide IT administrations supplier.

TCS's development was driven by a promise to quality and development. The organization extended its administrations to include application advancement, programming support, and IT counseling. It embraced a worldwide viewpoint from the beginning, with its most memorable global agreement gotten in 1974 with the Unified Domains based organization, Burroughs Company.

The organization's excursion towards turning into a worldwide IT goliath went on through the 1990s when it became one of the main Indian IT organizations to lay out a presence in the US. TCS profited by the developing interest for IT re-appropriating and laid out seaward advancement communities to actually serve clients.

TCS's client-centered approach and obligation to greatness put it aside. It underlined constructing long haul associations with clients, a technique that has added to its development and notoriety. TCS became known for its devotion to quality, reflected in its adherence to industry principles and confirmations. It got the ISO 9001 certificate in 1992, making it one of the primary Indian organizations to accomplish this acknowledgment.

Throughout the long term, TCS expanded its administrations to take care of different industry verticals, including banking, monetary administrations, protection, retail, medical services, and assembling. Its abilities in big business arrangements, distributed computing, and information examination further extended its portfolio.

TCS additionally embraced the idea of the worldwide conveyance model, permitting it to furnish clients with practical and effective administrations. The organization's labor force developed dramatically, and it became eminent for its accentuation on ability improvement and preparing. It laid out the TCS Institute, a committed instructional hub for representatives, and carried out various drives to encourage development and business venture.

TCS's obligation to manageability and corporate social obligation is apparent through its endeavors to diminish its carbon impression, advance variety and incorporation, and backing social and local area drives. It has reliably positioned among the top IT administrations organizations around the world and has gotten various honors and acknowledgments for its commitments to the business.

Infosys:

Infosys, established in 1981 by N. R. Narayana Murthy and a gathering of six designers, arose as a trailblazer in India's IT industry. The organization's foundation denoted a critical achievement in the country's IT process as it became one of the soonest IT administrations organizations to zero in on programming improvement and counseling administrations.

Infosys' process started with an unassuming speculation of just $250, which the pioneers acquired from their mates. In spite of its modest starting points, the organization was based on a groundwork of solid qualities, including a pledge to client fulfillment, greatness, and moral strategic policies.

Infosys immediately acquired a standing for its commitment to quality and innovation development. The organization's work in programming advancement and counseling administrations pulled in clients in India and abroad.

Its initial clients remembered large companies for the US and Europe, denoting its progress from a startup to a worldwide IT administrations supplier.

The organization's first sale of stock (Initial public offering) in 1993 was a defining moment, as it turned into the main Indian organization to be recorded on NASDAQ. This noticeable the start of Infosys' excursion as a public corporation, prompting huge extension and development.

Infosys' accentuation on worker government assistance and strengthening has been a sign of its way of life. The organization's open and cooperative workplace, alongside a solid spotlight on preparing and improvement, has permitted it to draw in and hold top ability in the business. Infosys made its own schooling and preparing focus, Infosys Preparing Center, to furnish representatives with the abilities and information expected to succeed in their jobs.

The worldwide conveyance model turned into an essential piece of Infosys' tasks, permitting it to proficiently serve global clients and give savvy arrangements. The organization extended its administrations to cover different spaces, including finance, retail, assembling, medical services, and broadcast communications.

Infosys has reliably been at the bleeding edge of innovation patterns, embracing regions, for example, man-made brainpower, distributed computing, and computerized change. It has utilized these progressions to assist clients with adjusting to developing business sector requests and stay serious.

One of the central qualities of Infosys is its obligation to corporate administration, straightforwardness, and moral strategic approaches. The organization's emphasis on manageability and social obligation is clear through its endeavors to diminish its carbon impression, support instruction and medical services drives, and advance variety and consideration inside its labor force.

Wipro:

Wipro, short for Western India Items, was established in 1945 as a producer of vegetable and refined oils in Amalner, Maharashtra. It was at first an unassuming business run by Mohamed Premji, who later gave over control to his child, Azim Premji, in 1966. Azim Premji's entrance denoted a critical change for the organization, as he perceived the potential in expanding its tasks.

In 1980, Wipro wandered into the IT business, beginning with the creation of smaller than expected PCs and other equipment. It fostered its most memorable PC in 1981 and was quite possibly the earliest

Indian organization to fabricate PCs. Wipro's initial introduction to IT laid the basis for its development into an extensive IT administrations supplier.

Wipro's excursion in the IT area included a two dimensional methodology. The organization at first centered around equipment assembling and frameworks incorporation. It fostered a standing for creating solid equipment frameworks, including minicomputers, workstations, and servers, which were utilized by different organizations and government associations.

In the mid 1990s, Wipro extended its administrations to incorporate programming advancement and IT administrations. It started to give application improvement and support, frameworks coordination, and counseling administrations to a different arrangement of clients. This shift denoted the organization's change into the worldwide IT administrations field.

Wipro's obligation to quality and advancement was obvious in its product improvement endeavors. The organization put resources into innovative work, laid out a devoted programming improvement focus, and stressed the significance of sticking to industry guidelines and best practices.

Wipro's worldwide conveyance model permitted it to proficiently serve clients around the world, giving savvy and top notch arrangements. The organization extended its administrations to take care of many enterprises, including finance, medical services, retail, and media communications.

The organization's emphasis on representative strengthening and improvement made a flourishing work culture. Wipro put resources into preparing and expertise improvement, encouraging development and a culture of ceaseless improvement. It laid out the Wipro Way of thinking to advance scholarly capital and animate inventiveness among representatives.

Wipro's obligation to maintainability and corporate obligation is apparent through its endeavors to decrease its natural effect, advance variety and consideration, and participate in friendly and local area drives. The organization has reliably positioned as one of the top IT administrations suppliers worldwide and has been perceived for its commitments to the business.

The Enormous Three's Effect on the Indian IT Industry:

TCS, Infosys, and Wipro by and large structure the foundation of the Indian IT industry and play played critical parts in forming its advancement. Their commitments to the business can be summed up as follows:

Spearheading Worldwide Administrations: TCS, Infosys, and Wipro were among the earliest Indian IT organizations to offer worldwide IT administrations. They exhibited the capability of Indian IT ability to convey excellent administrations to clients around the world.

Worldwide Conveyance Model: These organizations promoted the worldwide conveyance model, which includes conveying IT administrations from seaward areas. This model diminished costs for clients as well as empowered effective and nonstop help.

Accentuation on Quality: The Huge Three have reliably kept an emphasis on quality, procuring certificates and sticking to industry guidelines. This obligation to greatness has been a foundation of their prosperity.

Labor force Improvement: TCS, Infosys, and Wipro have put altogether in worker preparing and advancement. They have made learning and improvement focuses to outfit their labor force with the fundamental abilities to succeed in the IT business.

4.3 The role of IT in shaping India's digital and economic future.

The job of Data Innovation (IT) in molding India's computerized and financial future couldn't possibly be more significant. Throughout the course of recent many years, India has taken huge steps in the IT area, changing itself into a worldwide innovation center and a vital participant in the computerized economy. This change has achieved monetary development as well as had significant ramifications for different parts of Indian culture.

The Computerized Upset in India:

The computerized upset in India started in the late twentieth hundred years, with the development of the IT business as a main impetus. The progression of the Indian economy in the mid 1990s assumed an essential part in cultivating a climate helpful for IT development. It opened ways to unfamiliar venture, facilitated guidelines, and urged innovation organizations to set up activities in India.

The IT area immediately picked up speed and advanced into a diverse industry, including programming improvement, IT administrations, business process rethinking (BPO), and information process re-appropriating (KPO). The country's standing for giving top notch IT administrations at a cutthroat expense prompted the rethinking of IT and business processes by worldwide organizations, a pattern that proceeds right up 'til now.

The Indian government additionally perceived the significance of the IT area in molding the country's computerized future. Drives, for example, "Computerized India" were sent off to advance the utilization of innovation and advanced framework to upgrade taxpayer supported organizations, availability, and computerized proficiency among residents.

The Computerized India drive has been instrumental in achieving a scope of advanced administrations, including e-administration, advanced installments, and versatile applications. These administrations have worked on the proficiency of government tasks as well as enabled residents by giving them admittance to taxpayer supported organizations easily.

Moreover, the coming of the Aadhaar project, an interesting biometric ID framework, has upset character confirmation and admittance to government benefits. It has empowered monetary incorporation, as a great many unbanked residents have accessed financial administrations through computerized stages.

Financial Development and Occupation Creation:

The IT business in India plays had a huge impact in supporting the country's monetary development. India's IT and IT-empowered administrations area has reliably contributed a significant portion of the country's Total national output (Gross domestic product). These commitments have been supported by the business' ceaseless development, both concerning income and work age.

The IT area has made huge number of occupations in India, straightforwardly utilizing a tremendous labor force containing programming designers, project supervisors, examiners, and care staff. Also, it has by implication created work open doors in related areas, including land, neighborliness, transportation, and retail, as innovation center points and IT parks have prompted urbanization and financial advancement in different urban areas.

Besides, its development has prompted the improvement of particular instructive establishments and preparing focuses, like Indian Organizations of Innovation (IITs) and programming preparing schools, which get ready people for IT professions. This has been instrumental in diminishing joblessness and upgrading the abilities of the Indian labor force.

The IT business' worldwide conveyance model, which consolidates nearby and seaward turn of events, has assisted global clients with getting to financially savvy administrations while likewise giving work open doors in India. Indian IT organizations have gained notoriety for offering top notch administrations, and their customers has extended to remember worldwide companies for different businesses, from money and medical care to assembling and retail.

Engaging Business people and New companies:
The IT area in India has not just determined the development of laid out IT goliaths yet has likewise given a ripe ground to new companies and business visionaries. India has seen a prospering startup biological system, especially in innovation related fields like web based business, fintech, healthtech, and edtech.

Hatcheries, gas pedals, and funding firms play had a huge impact in supporting the development of new companies. They give assets, mentorship, and financing to promising business people, empowering them to transform inventive thoughts into fruitful organizations. Thus, India has seen the rise of unicorns, new companies esteemed at more than a billion bucks, in different areas, demonstrating the profundity and variety of pioneering ability.

The Indian government has likewise acquainted a few drives with advance business and development. "Startup India" is one such program pointed toward establishing a climate that cultivates and upholds new businesses. It offers advantages like expense exceptions, more straightforward admittance to subsidizing, and worked on guidelines to empower the development of new organizations.

Advanced Change Across Areas:

IT plays had a significant impact in empowering computerized change across different areas in India. Here are a few key regions where this change has been especially critical:

Medical services: Advanced wellbeing arrangements, telemedicine, and electronic wellbeing records have worked on tolerant consideration and medical care access. Advancements like man-made consciousness (simulated intelligence) and information examination are utilized for illness determination, drug disclosure, and prescient medical care.

Schooling: The digitalization of training has prompted e-learning stages, online course contributions, and intelligent instructive assets. It has made quality schooling open to a more extensive populace and worked with long lasting learning.

Monetary Administrations: The fintech area has seen huge development, with advanced installments, versatile banking, and online venture stages becoming fundamental to the monetary scene. Monetary incorporation has been a key driver, giving admittance to banking administrations to the unbanked and underbanked populace.

Agribusiness: IT arrangements have been utilized to work on agrarian practices, crop the executives, and market access for ranchers.

Computerized stages give climate data, market costs, and warning administrations to improve efficiency and decrease gambles.

E-Administration: Taxpayer driven organizations are progressively open internet, improving on authoritative cycles and decreasing regulatory formality. Residents can get to administrations, for example, applying for ID archives, making good on duties, and following government projects effortlessly.

Shrewd Urban communities: The idea of savvy urban communities includes utilizing IT to upgrade metropolitan preparation, framework, and administrations. These drives mean to make reasonable, effective, and bearable metropolitan conditions.

Framework and Network:

India's advanced and financial future is intently attached to its endeavors to grow computerized framework and network. The development of the web, versatile organizations, and broadband administrations has been fundamental in associating remote and underserved regions to the advanced biological system.

The rollout of 4G and 5G organizations, alongside drives like "BharatNet," which plans to give broadband network to rustic regions, can possibly carry computerized administrations to a more extensive populace. Improved availability opens up open doors for advanced instruction, web based business, telemedicine, and taxpayer driven organizations, adding to monetary development and social turn of events.

Difficulties and Amazing open doors:

While the IT area in India has made amazing progress, it keeps on confronting different difficulties and valuable open doors that will shape its job in the nation's computerized and financial future:

Abilities Hole: The fast development of innovation requires a gifted labor force fit for adjusting to new turns of events. Crossing over the abilities hole and upgrading advanced education is fundamental to guarantee that the labor force stays serious and important in the computerized period.

Network protection: As India's advanced biological system extends, the significance of online protection develops. Safeguarding basic foundation, information, and individual data from digital dangers is a huge test that should be addressed to keep up with trust and security in the computerized climate.

Security and Information Assurance: Information security and insurance guidelines are turning out to be progressively critical, and India has presented the Individual Information Security Bill to address these worries. Laying out strong information security measures is fundamental for cultivating trust in computerized administrations.

Inclusivity: Growing advanced admittance to all portions of the populace, including underestimated networks, is basic for guaranteeing that the advantages of the computerized economy are generally conveyed.

Development and Exploration: Empowering examination and development in arising innovations like computer based intelligence, blockchain, and quantum figuring is fundamental to keep up with India's situation as a worldwide innovation pioneer.

Natural Manageability: The IT area's development should be off-set with ecological maintainability. Energy-productive advancements, green server farms, and capable e-squander the board are regions where the business can add to manageability objectives.

Worldwide Rivalry: The worldwide IT scene is profoundly serious, with nations like China and the US additionally competing for authority in the advanced economy. India should proceed to enhance and stay serious to get its spot in the worldwide market.

5

Chapter 5

Contemporary Industrial Titans

In the cutting edge world, where innovation and globalization have reshaped the scene of industry and business, contemporary modern titans have arisen as compelling and strong elements. These goliaths of the business world employ monstrous impact over economies, social orders, and even states, frequently forming the course of history itself. While the expression "modern titan" has developed over the long run to incorporate a great many areas and enterprises, this exposition will investigate the idea of contemporary modern titans, their effect on the world, and the elements that have added to their ascent.

Contemporary modern titans are in many cases portrayed by their predominance in different areas, their immense assets, and their capacity to shape markets and social orders. They are normally global organizations with a presence in various nations, and their tasks length a wide cluster of enterprises. The absolute most conspicuous names in this class incorporate organizations like Apple, Amazon, Google (Letter set), Facebook (Meta), Microsoft, and Tesla, among others.

One of the key elements that recognizes these contemporary modern titans is their effect on the worldwide economy. Their market capitalization frequently surpasses the Gross domestic product of numerous nations, giving them a significant monetary presence. These organizations are significant businesses as well as huge supporters of the expense base of the nations in which they work. This financial impact reaches out to supply chains, as they frequently work with a tremendous organization of providers and accomplices, further establishing their status as monetary behemoths.

The ascent of these contemporary modern titans can be credited to a few elements. Innovative progressions play had a critical influence, permitting these organizations to disturb conventional ventures and make new business sectors. The approach of the web, the multiplication of cell phones, and the development of internet business have all given prolific ground to the extension of these organizations. They have utilized innovation to smooth out their activities as well as to foster creative items and administrations that have changed how we live, work, and impart.

Notwithstanding innovation, the business procedures utilized by these titans have been instrumental in their rising. They have embraced a mix of forceful extension, consolidations and acquisitions, and vital speculations. This has permitted them to broaden their item and administration contributions, enter new business sectors, and cement their situation as industry pioneers. The quest for economies of scale and degree has been a main thrust behind their development, empowering them to convey labor and products at serious costs.

Besides, their capacity to bridle information and influence computerized reasoning (man-made intelligence) has given them a huge edge. Information has turned into a significant asset, and these organizations have become skilled at gathering, investigating, and adapting it. Their computer based intelligence abilities empower them to give customized suggestions, upgrade client encounters, and streamline their tasks. This information driven approach has worked on their main concerns as well as developed their impact over customer conduct and direction.

One more basic part of their prosperity is their worldwide reach. These organizations have extended past their home business sectors, catching a worldwide client base. Their capacity to adjust their items and administrations to different social and monetary settings has been a vital figure their global achievement. This worldwide presence has expanded their income as well as upgraded their political and monetary impact, as they explore the intricacies of various administrative conditions and government relations.

Be that as it may, the development and impact of contemporary modern titans have not been without discussion. As they have filled in size and power, worries about their effect on society have strengthened. These worries length a large number of issues, including syndication power, protection, work rehearses, natural effect, and tax collection. The strength of certain organizations in their separate businesses has raised worries about fair rivalry and the potential for monopolistic way of behaving, with some contending for stricter antitrust guidelines.

The assortment and utilization of immense measures of client information by these organizations have raised security worries, with inquiries concerning how this information is put away, shared, and protected. Issues connected with information breaks and the potential for information abuse have filled public and administrative investigation. Moreover, worries about the work rehearses inside these organizations have come to the very front, as inquiries regarding specialist conditions, wages, and employer stability have been raised. This has prompted expanded requests for fair treatment of representatives and more straightforward corporate obligation.

Natural worries have likewise arisen, especially on account of organizations engaged with the creation and appropriation of actual items. The carbon impression and ecological effect of these tasks have gone under investigation, and there is a developing call for additional economical practices and a pledge to decreasing ozone harming substance outflows. As consciousness of environmental change and natural debasement develops, modern titans are progressively being considered responsible for their part in these difficulties.

Tax collection is one more petulant issue, with worries about charge evasion procedures utilized by a portion of these organizations. The utilization of seaward assessment shelters and other monetary moves has started banters about their commitment to public expense income. State run administrations have been feeling the squeeze to resolve these issues and guarantee that organizations pay their reasonable portion of assessments.

The political impact of contemporary modern titans is one more subject of discussion. Their monetary power frequently converts into political power, as they campaign legislatures and take part in political exercises that line up with their inclinations. This impact can shape strategy choices, administrative systems, and even decisions, raising worries about the expected mutilation of vote based processes.

The discussion about the impact of contemporary modern titans reaches out past their monetary and political power and addresses more extensive cultural and social angles. These organizations have become critical players in forming mainstream society and the manner in which individuals convey, collaborate, and consume data. They have adjusted the media scene, with the ascent of advanced stages affecting conventional news coverage and news sources. Virtual entertainment has turned into a prevailing power in molding public talk, and these organizations assume a vital part in figuring out what content contacts a worldwide crowd.

The manner in which contemporary modern titans handle issues of content control, falsehood, and the harmony between free discourse and the anticipation of damage has additionally created huge public conversation. The ability to shape general assessment and the possibility to enhance or smother voices have led to banters about oversight and the obligation of these organizations to control content on their foundation.

In spite of the contentions and discussions encompassing contemporary modern titans, it is obvious that they have reformed different parts of our lives. The accommodations and developments they have brought to society have made them necessary to our everyday schedules. We depend on their items and administrations for correspondence, diversion, data, and, surprisingly, fundamental necessities. The accommodation of internet shopping, the network of virtual entertainment, and the extraordinary abilities of cell phones are developments driven by these organizations.

Moreover, they have been at the very front of innovative work in regions like man-made reasoning, environmentally friendly power, and space investigation. Their interests in state of the art advances can possibly address probably the most squeezing worldwide difficulties, from environmental change to medical care. These undertakings feature their capacity to drive advancement as well as feature their ability to handle great, complex issues.

In the field of environmentally friendly power, for instance, organizations like Tesla have pushed the limits of electric vehicle innovation and have gained ground in practical energy creation. These endeavors are basic in the worldwide progress toward an additional earth capable and reasonable future.

One more region in which contemporary modern titans have made significant commitments is medical care. The utilization of man-made intelligence and huge information in clinical examination and diagnostics can possibly change medical care conveyance, making it more proficient and available. Organizations like Google and Amazon have entered the medical care space, looking to use their innovative ability to work on persistent results and decrease the expense of medical care.

The venture into space investigation is one more illustration of their spearheading endeavors. Organizations like SpaceX, established by Elon Musk, are endeavoring to diminish the expense of room travel and at last empower human colonization of different planets. These aggressive objectives are energizing by their own doing as well as connote the readiness of these organizations to wander into new boondocks.

The humanitarian endeavors of a few contemporary modern titans are likewise imperative. A large number of these organizations are engaged with magnanimous work and social drives, resolving issues like schooling, medical care, neediness mitigation, and debacle help. The colossal abundance created by their prosperity has empowered them to make huge commitments to worthy missions.

The impact of these titans stretches out to the startup environment also. They frequently put resources into and gain promising new companies, furnishing them with the assets and mentorship expected to develop and flourish. This cultivates development as well as assists arising organizations with accessing .

5.1 In-depth look at modern industrial giants like Reliance Industries and the Adani Group.

In the consistently developing scene of worldwide industry and business, certain corporate elements stand apart as present day modern goliaths that fundamentally affect their particular ventures and the more extensive economy. Two such conspicuous combinations in India are Dependence Ventures and the Adani Gathering. In this thorough investigation, we will dig into these modern behemoths, looking at their set of experiences, key business areas, influence on the Indian and worldwide economies, as well as the difficulties and potential open doors they face in this day and age.

Dependence Businesses, established by Dhirubhai Ambani in 1966, has arisen as one of the biggest and most enhanced combinations in India. The organization's process started with material assembling and steadily ventured into petrochemicals, refining, broadcast communications, retail, and advanced administrations. Today, under the administration of Mukesh Ambani, Dhirubhai's child, Dependence Ventures has developed to envelop a wide exhibit of organizations, each assuming a huge part in India's financial scene.

The energy area is where Dependence Businesses at first did something significant. The organization claims the world's biggest single-area processing plant complex in Jamnagar, Gujarat, with a refining limit that surpasses 1.2 million barrels each day. This broad refining limit has not just made India confident in oil based commodities yet in addition transformed the country into a significant exporter of refined petrol. Dependence's Jamnagar processing plant is known for its mechanical greatness and functional productivity.

Dependence's introduction to the petrochemicals area has likewise been a distinct advantage. The organization's Jamnagar complex is one of the world's biggest petrochemical fabricating center points, delivering many items, including polymers, polyesters, and synthetics. This broadening has fortified the organization's portfolio as well as contributed altogether to India's petrochemical industry's development.

Another basic area where Dependence Ventures has made a permanent imprint is media communications. The send off of Dependence Jio Infocomm in 2016 upset the Indian telecom market. Under Mukesh Ambani's initiative, Dependence Jio presented reasonable information and voice plans, driving advanced consideration and changing the manner in which Indians impart and get to the web. This imaginative methodology prompted a monstrous supporter base for Jio in a brief period, making it one of the biggest telecom administrators in India.

Moreover, the retail area has been a point of convergence of Dependence's broadening endeavors. Dependence Retail has extended quickly, offering many items and administrations, from food to gadgets and design. The securing of laid out corporate store, like Future Gathering's resources, has fortified Dependence's presence in this area and solidified its status as an imposing player in the retail business.

Dependence Enterprises has likewise wandered into the computerized administrations space with Jio Stages, which offers a set-up of applications, advanced content, and advanced installments. The reconciliation of Jio's media communications framework with computerized administrations has made a comprehensive environment, further improving client commitment and market entrance.

The effect of Dependence Ventures on the Indian economy is unquestionable. The organization's commitments to the energy area, petrochemicals, and broadcast communications have pushed India towards independence as well as powered financial development. It has made positions, supported trades, and aided span the computerized partition by making reasonable internet providers open to a huge populace.

Furthermore, Dependence's aggressive drives have gathered critical unfamiliar ventures. High-profile ventures from organizations like Facebook, Google, and others in Jio Stages exhibit the worldwide premium in the Indian market and its true capacity for remarkable development.

Notwithstanding, as a corporate goliath with an extensive impact, Dependence Businesses faces its portion of difficulties. One of the essential difficulties is the need to keep up with consistence with administrative and antitrust regulations, particularly considering its different business property and market predominance in specific areas.

Also, the telecom area's hyper-cutthroat nature has prompted estimating pressures and required persistent interests in foundation and development. The need to support and develop Jio's endorser base and computerized administrations presents a continuous test.

In the retail area, Dependence faces rivalry from both homegrown and worldwide players. The retail business is profoundly unique, and remaining ahead as far as piece of the pie and client experience is a nonstop undertaking.

Another test is ecological and social obligation. The petrochemical and energy areas are under a magnifying glass for their ecological effect, and Dependence has sincerely committed to supportability and decreasing its carbon impression. Offsetting monetary development with natural obligation is a test looked by numerous modern monsters.

Conversely, the Adani Gathering, drove by very rich person Gautam Adani, has arisen as one more modern goliath in India. The gathering's development direction has been striking, and it presently brags a different portfolio organizations, including framework, energy, operations, and assets.

One of the center qualities of the Adani Gathering lies in the foundation area. The gathering has put vigorously in building and working ports, air terminals, and power transmission projects.

The Mundra Port in Gujarat, quite possibly of India's biggest business port, is a demonstration of the gathering's obligation to foundation improvement. It has added to the simplicity of carrying on with work in India and the help of global exchange.

The energy area is one more huge center region for the Adani Gathering. The gathering has a significant presence in both warm and environmentally friendly power age. The Mundra Nuclear energy Station is one of the biggest coal-based power plants in India, producing a significant piece of Gujarat's power supply. Furthermore, the gathering has made significant interests in environmentally friendly power, with a developing arrangement of sun based and wind energy projects. This obligation to environmentally friendly power lines up with the worldwide shift towards cleaner energy sources and manageability.

The Adani Gathering has likewise made advances into the operations area, with Adani Ports and Extraordinary Monetary Zone (APSEZ) assuming a urgent part. The obtaining of different ports and the improvement of coordinated operations foundation have situated the gathering as a central participant in the strategies and transportation space.

Besides, the gathering has interests in normal assets, including coal mining and exchanging. Adani Endeavors Restricted (AEL) is the gathering's leader organization in this area. It plays had a critical impact in the import and exchanging of coal for different ventures, including power age.

Gautam Adani's vision for the gathering reaches out past India. The Adani Gathering has put resources into tasks and resources in different nations, including Australia, Indonesia, and Africa. These worldwide speculations have extended the gathering's worldwide impression as well as reinforced India's monetary binds with different countries.

The effect of the Adani Gathering on the Indian economy is significant. Its interests in foundation, energy, and coordinated operations have made positions, animated financial development, and further developed the country's business climate. The gathering's obligation to environmentally friendly power lines up with India's objectives of diminishing fossil fuel byproducts and progressing to a supportable energy future.

Notwithstanding, the Adani Gathering has additionally confronted its portion of difficulties. One of the fundamental difficulties lies in dealing with the different areas in which it works. Broadening can be both a benefit and a test, as it requires compelling oversight and administration to guarantee every business portion flourishes.

Additionally, the gathering's extension and interests in basic areas, like energy and framework, require significant capital. Admittance to funding, both locally and universally, is a test that the gathering should explore really to help its development plans.

Administrative and natural worries are additionally areas of thought. The energy area, especially coal-based power age, is under a microscope for its ecological effect. Complying with ecological guidelines while guaranteeing energy security is a fragile equilibrium.

The opposition in the foundation and operations areas is furious, with other key part competing for a portion of the market. Remaining ahead as far as functional proficiency and administration quality is a steady test.

All in all, Dependence Ventures and the Adani Gathering are present day modern goliaths in India that have made significant commitments to the country's monetary development and advancement. Dependence's broadened business portfolio traverses energy, petrochemicals, broadcast communications, retail, and computerized administrations, while the Adani Gathering succeeds in framework, energy, coordinated operations, and assets. The two combinations have put vigorously in different areas, making position, animating monetary development, and supporting India's situation on the worldwide stage.

While the two organizations have experienced their individual difficulties, like administrative consistence, market rivalry, and ecological worries, their visionary chiefs, Mukesh Ambani and Gautam Adani, have exhibited a wonderful capacity to adjust and enhance. These modern goliaths are changing their particular businesses as well as molding the fate of India's monetary scene. As they proceed to advance and expand, their effect on India's development and improvement is supposed to stay huge.

5.2 Their diversified interests and contributions to various sectors.

The achievement and effect of present day modern goliaths like Dependence Ventures and the Adani Gathering stretch out past their differentiated advantages, venturing into numerous areas and essentially adding to India's economy and worldwide business scene. The two combinations have shown exceptional flexibility and versatility, and their interests in different areas have created significant financial development and work valuable open doors. This article investigates their enhanced advantages and commitments to various areas.

Dependence Enterprises, under the initiative of Mukesh Ambani, has turned into a quintessential illustration of broadening and key development. The combination's advantages range a variety of areas, each assuming a special part in forming India's monetary scene.

The energy area has generally been a center concentration for Dependence. The organization works the world's biggest single-area refining complex in Jamnagar, Gujarat, with a refining limit surpassing 1.2 million barrels each day. This noteworthy foundation has situated India as a vital participant in the worldwide refining industry, decreasing its reliance on oil based good imports and empowering huge products. The Jamnagar treatment facility is famous for its functional effectiveness and mechanical greatness, setting industry benchmarks in process advancement and efficiency.

Dependence's introduction to petrochemicals has been similarly noteworthy. Its Jamnagar complex isn't just a refining center point yet in addition one of the world's biggest petrochemical producing focuses. The development of an extensive variety of petrochemical items, including polymers, polyesters, and synthetic compounds, has essentially added to India's petrochemical industry. These items are essential to different enterprises, from bundling and materials to car and purchaser products, assisting India's independence and supporting the country's assembling capacities.

The combination's enhancement into the broadcast communications area with the send off of Dependence Jio Infocomm in 2016 was a game-evolving move. Jio disturbed the Indian telecom market by offering reasonable information and voice plans, really democratizing admittance to rapid web and portable administrations. The move sped up India's computerized change, spanning the metropolitan provincial advanced partition and empowering millions to get to the web and computerized administrations. Thus, Dependence Jio quickly amassed one of the biggest endorser bases in the nation, making it a prevailing player in the telecom business.

Retail is another area where Dependence Ventures has made critical advances. Dependence Retail, the combination's retail arm, has encountered fast development, offering a wide range of items and administrations, from food to gadgets and design. The procurement of laid out corporate store, like Future Gathering's resources, has fortified Dependence's situation in this area and hardened its status as a considerable player in Indian retail. The combination's abundant resources and assets have empowered it to put resources into modernizing and growing the retail business, making a consistent shopping experience for clients.

Dependence Enterprises' advanced administrations arm, Jio Stages, has taken huge steps in the computerized space. Jio Stages gives a set-up of applications, computerized content, and advanced installment administrations, offering an extensive environment for customers. The mix of Jio's broadcast communications foundation with computerized administrations has upset the manner in which Indians access advanced content, convey, and take part in web-based exercises. This cooperative energy improves client commitment and market entrance while advancing a computerized first culture in the country.

The differentiated interests of Dependence Ventures are not restricted to these areas alone. The combination has made key interests in areas like medical care and training. Through Dependence Establishment, the organization has started different generous projects, zeroing in on medical services, schooling, and catastrophe help. These drives highlight the organization's obligation to social obligation and adding to the prosperity of the local area.

The Adani Gathering, drove by Gautam Adani, is one more modern monster with different interests that have made a permanent imprint on different areas.

Foundation improvement has been a foundation of the Adani Gathering's broadening endeavors. The gathering has put altogether in building and working ports, air terminals, and power transmission projects. Mundra Port in Gujarat, perhaps of India's biggest business port, represents the gathering's commitment to framework advancement. It plays had an essential impact in working with worldwide exchange, upgrading India's worldwide network, and working on the simplicity of carrying on with work in the country.

The energy area is one more point of convergence for the Adani Gathering. The gathering has laid out a vigorous presence in both warm and environmentally friendly power age. The Mundra Nuclear energy Station, one of India's biggest coal-based power plants, contributes essentially to Gujarat's power supply. The gathering has likewise made significant interests in environmentally friendly power, with a developing arrangement of sunlight based and wind energy projects. These speculations line up with the worldwide shift toward cleaner energy sources and supportable practices.

The planned operations area is a critical area of concentration for the Adani Gathering, with Adani Ports and Exceptional Monetary Zone (APSEZ) as the main thrust. The gathering's essential acquisitions and improvement of coordinated factors foundation have situated it as a central part in the planned operations and transportation industry. This broad organization of ports and transportation offices improves exchange and trade, encouraging India's situation as a worldwide business center point.

Regular assets, explicitly coal mining and exchanging, additionally fall inside the Adani Gathering's differentiated advantages. Adani Ventures Restricted (AEL), the gathering's lead organization in this area, plays had a huge impact in the import and exchanging of coal, serving different businesses, including power age.

Gautam Adani's vision for the gathering stretches out past India. The Adani Gathering has wandered into worldwide business sectors, making interests in tasks and resources in nations like Australia, Indonesia, and Africa. These worldwide speculations have extended the gathering's worldwide impression and reinforced India's monetary binds with different countries.

The commitments of the Adani Gathering to the Indian economy are significant. Its interests in foundation, energy, and operations have made positions, animated financial development, and further developed the country's business climate. The gathering's obligation to environmentally friendly power lines up with India's objectives of decreasing fossil fuel byproducts and progressing to a practical energy future.

Similarly as with Dependence Enterprises, the Adani Gathering likewise faces difficulties related with enhancement. Dealing with a combination with interests crossing numerous areas requires compelling oversight and administration to guarantee every business section flourishes and works in collaboration.

The development and interests in basic areas, like energy and framework, require significant capital. Guaranteeing admittance to funding, both locally and globally, is a test that the gathering should explore really to help its development plans.

Administrative and natural worries are areas of thought, especially in the energy area, which is under a microscope for its ecological effect. Offsetting natural guidelines with energy security is a perplexing undertaking.

Rivalry in the framework and operations areas is wild, with other central parts competing for a portion of the market. Remaining ahead as far as functional productivity and administration quality is a steady test that requires progressing development and speculation.

Both Dependence Businesses and the Adani Gathering share a guarantee to manageability and corporate social obligation. The accentuation on natural obligation and local area prosperity is basic as these aggregates proceed to extend and broaden.

Moreover, these modern monsters have been at the front line of mechanical advancement. On account of Dependence Businesses, its computerized administrations arm, Jio Stages, is a perfect representation. By coordinating broadcast communications framework with computerized administrations, Jio has reformed the manner in which individuals in India access the web and advanced content. This advanced change has further developed availability as well as opened up new open doors for organizations and people, especially with regards to internet business, online training, and computerized diversion.

Likewise, the Adani Gathering's interests in environmentally friendly power line up with India's yearnings to decrease fossil fuel byproducts and progress toward a manageable energy future. By integrating sun powered and wind energy projects into their portfolio, the Adani Gathering isn't simply adding to the country's energy security yet in addition progressing natural manageability.

Notwithstanding mechanical advancement and manageability, the two combinations are profoundly dedicated to humanitarian endeavors. Dependence Ventures, through Dependence Establishment, and the Adani Gathering, through the Adani Establishment, have sent off various social and local area improvement drives. These endeavors center around medical care, training, calamity help, and other basic regions, adding to the prosperity of society and highlighting the significance of corporate social obligation.

The expanded interests and commitments of Dependence Ventures and the Adani Gathering reach out to different areas, making a complex effect on India's economy and society. These combinations have changed ventures, gave occupations, sped up computerized incorporation, further developed framework, and driven supportable practices. Their visionary initiative and versatility .

5.3 Their role in driving innovation, employment, and economic growth.

The job of present day modern goliaths like Dependence Enterprises and the Adani Gathering reaches out a long ways past their broadened advantages; it envelops their crucial job in driving development, work, and financial development in India. The two combinations have been at the cutting edge of mechanical headways, cultivating advancement, creating significant work valuable open doors, and essentially adding to the country's financial turn of events.

Dependence Businesses, under the visionary authority of Mukesh Ambani, has been a main impetus behind development in different areas. The aggregate's obligation to mechanical progression has been especially articulated in the broadcast communications area through Dependence Jio Infocomm.

The send off of Dependence Jio in 2016 denoted a groundbreaking second in India's media communications industry. The presentation of reasonable information and voice plans disturbed the market, making fast web and versatile administrations open to an expansive range of the populace. Dependence Jio's essential way to deal with evaluating and framework advancement prompted dramatic development in supporters, making it one of the biggest telecom administrators in India.

Jio's development went past moderateness; it prodded contest and advancement across the area. The far reaching influence of Jio's entrance into the market provoked other telecom administrators to upgrade their administrations and put resources into growing their organizations. This serious climate supported innovative headways and further developed help quality, helping purchasers and the general broadcast communications industry.

Moreover, Dependence Jio's emphasis on 4G innovation and its nonstop interests in 5G foundation have situated India to be at the very front of the worldwide broadcast communications scene. The push toward 5G availability won't just further lift web speeds yet additionally open up additional opportunities in regions like the Web of Things (IoT), brilliant urban areas, and advanced medical care.

In the retail area, Dependence Ventures has likewise been a harbinger of development. The securing of laid out corporate store and the mix of innovation into retail tasks have changed the area. Dependence Retail's accentuation on digitalization has further developed store network the board, stock control, and client experience. The combination's endeavors to smooth out tasks significantly affect the retail business, inciting contenders to take on comparable practices to stay serious.

The computerized administrations arm, Jio Stages, has likewise determined development in the advanced area. The set-up of applications and computerized content administrations presented by Jio Stages has had an impact on the manner in which Indians access and associate with advanced content. The coordination of computerized administrations with broadcast communications foundation has made a comprehensive computerized biological system, upgrading client commitment and market entrance.

Dependence Businesses' introduction to environmentally friendly power is one more demonstration of its obligation to development. The organization has made huge interests in sun based and wind energy projects, adding to India's objectives of diminishing fossil fuel byproducts and progressing to cleaner energy sources. These interests in sustainable power are ecologically dependable as well as address a forward-looking way to deal with energy creation.

On account of the Adani Gathering, Gautam Adani's vision for advancement has prompted critical improvements in the energy area. The gathering's interests in warm and environmentally friendly power age have achieved significant progressions. The Mundra Nuclear energy Station, one of the biggest coal-based power plants in India, is a great representation of how the gathering has used imaginative innovation and cycles to upgrade power age. The plant's functional effectiveness and ecological consistence have set industry norms.

Furthermore, the Adani Gathering's obligation to sustainable power lines up with India's objectives of lessening fossil fuel byproducts and accomplishing energy security. By putting resources into sun based and wind energy projects, the gathering has added to maintainable energy creation as well as animated mechanical advancements in the environmentally friendly power area. These drives have likewise made ready for the advancement of effective energy stockpiling and dissemination frameworks, fundamental for the development of the environmentally friendly power industry.

In the strategies area, the Adani Gathering plays had a crucial impact in reforming port and transportation tasks through the turn of events and development of Mundra Port and other operations foundation. The reconciliation of innovation and robotization in port tasks has further developed productivity and freight taking care of limit. Moreover, the gathering's interests in holder terminals, strategies parks, and multi-modal transportation have worked with consistent exchange and store network activities.

Notwithstanding mechanical developments, the two aggregates have made critical commitments to monetary development and work in India. Dependence Enterprises and the Adani Gathering have made a large number of occupations across their different business areas, from energy and foundation to retail and media communications.

Dependence's broad organization of activities has created business open doors in different fields, from designing and assembling to advanced administrations and retail. The Jamnagar treatment facility and petrochemical complex alone utilize an enormous labor force, and the extension of Jio Stages, Dependence Retail, and computerized administrations has additionally expanded business possibilities.

The Adani Gathering's foundation speculations have prompted work creation in the development and activity of ports, air terminals, and power projects. The Mundra Port, with its huge freight taking care of limit, has powered business development in Gujarat. Additionally, the gathering's attention on environmentally friendly power has prompted work creation in the sun oriented and wind energy areas, as well as in coordinated operations and transportation.

The financial commitments of these modern goliaths are not restricted to coordinate business. Their ventures affect the economy. The improvement of framework, energy tasks, and retail tasks produces interest for a great many labor and products, in a roundabout way supporting organizations across different areas. This flowing impact animates financial development and helps in the advancement of subordinate businesses.

Moreover, the imaginative methodologies and computerized changes started by these combinations significantly affect India's enterprising scene. New companies and independent ventures have profited from the computerized foundation and administrations given by Dependence Enterprises and the Adani Gathering. The expanded openness of fast web, computerized installment arrangements, and web based business stages has engaged private ventures to arrive at a more extensive client base, extending their development potential.

The commitments of these combinations reach out to the advancement of abilities and human resources. Both Dependence Enterprises and the Adani Gathering have put resources into expertise advancement and preparing programs, for their representatives as well as for the more extensive local area. These drives upgrade employability as well as add to India's human resources improvement, cultivating a gifted labor force equipped for driving development and monetary development.

Dependence Enterprises and the Adani Gathering have likewise assumed a critical part in encouraging innovative work (Research and development). The mechanical progressions in the energy and framework areas, driven by these combinations, have set out open doors for

Research and development in regions like sustainable power, strategies, and media communications. This can possibly encourage a culture of development and advance the improvement of state of the art innovations in India.

Notwithstanding their immediate commitments to monetary development and advancement, the two combinations have shown areas of strength for a to corporate social obligation (CSR) and generosity. Dependence Ventures, through Dependence Establishment, and the Adani Gathering, through the Adani Establishment, have sent off various social and local area improvement drives. These drives center around medical care, training, catastrophe help, and other basic regions, adding to the prosperity of society and highlighting the significance of CSR.

Chapter 6

Pharma and Healthcare Powerhouses

Drug and medical care ventures are basic parts of a country's prosperity and progress. In this conversation, we'll dive into the drug and medical services forces to be reckoned with that have made huge commitments to worldwide wellbeing, research, and financial development. Two of the noticeable players in this space are Johnson and Johnson and Pfizer, the two of which have secured themselves as industry pioneers and assumed urgent parts in the turn of events and appropriation of medical care arrangements around the world.

Johnson and Johnson, a worldwide combination established in 1886, has developed into a worldwide forerunner in drugs, clinical gadgets, and buyer medical care items. Its obligation to development, patient consideration, and social obligation deserves it a merited standing as a medical services force to be reckoned with.

The drug arm of Johnson and Johnson, Janssen Drugs, has made significant commitments to the advancement of imaginative prescriptions and antibodies. The organization's innovative work endeavors length many restorative regions, from oncology and immunology to irresistible sicknesses and neuroscience. Strikingly, Janssen has been at the front line of investigation into therapies for illnesses with neglected clinical requirements, including HIV/Helps and tuberculosis. Its commitment to tending to worldwide wellbeing challenges is reflected in its associations with associations like the Worldwide Asset to Battle Helps, Tuberculosis, and Jungle fever.

Johnson and Johnson's obligation to patient prosperity stretches out to clinical gadgets, where it offers a variety of items intended to further develop medical services results. From careful instruments and muscular gadgets to cutting edge diagnostics and patient observing arrangements, the organization's clinical gadgets section assumes a pivotal part in improving patient consideration and supporting medical services experts.

In the customer medical care space, Johnson and Johnson has a vigorous arrangement of notable brands, like Neutrogena, Listerine, and Tylenol. These items give people admittance to over-the-counter cures, individual consideration things, and health arrangements that advance wellbeing and prosperity. The organization's obligation to quality and wellbeing is apparent in its devotion to straightforwardness and dependable promoting rehearses.

Past item improvement, Johnson and Johnson is effectively associated with worldwide wellbeing drives and generosity. The organization's associations with associations like the Bill and Melinda Doors Establishment and the World Wellbeing Association exhibit its obligation to tending to squeezing worldwide wellbeing challenges, especially in the space of maternal and kid wellbeing, irresistible sicknesses, and hunger.

Pfizer, another drug goliath, has a celebrated history tracing all the way back to 1849. The organization's obligation to medical services development and the improvement of life-saving meds and immunizations has made it a worldwide forerunner in the drug business. Pfizer's commitments to innovative work have yielded pivotal progressions in regions going from cardiovascular wellbeing to oncology and antibodies.

The turn of events and conveyance of immunizations have been a foundation of Pfizer's work. The organization plays had a significant impact in the improvement of immunizations for a great many illnesses, including pneumococcal sickness, meningitis, and, most as of late, Coronavirus. The organization among Pfizer and BioNTech prompted the production of one of the principal Coronavirus antibodies approved for crisis use. This great accomplishment significantly affects the worldwide reaction to the pandemic.

Pfizer's obligation to general wellbeing stretches out to its endeavors in illness counteraction and schooling. The organization has upheld drives zeroed in on tolerant training and medical care access, with a specific accentuation on further developing worldwide wellbeing results and tending to medical care variations.

Both Johnson and Johnson and Pfizer fundamentally affect monetary development, business, and innovative work. Their devotion to drug research has brought about the formation of life-saving prescriptions and antibodies, furnishing patients with fundamental medicines and further developing medical services results. The business open doors produced by these organizations range different fields, from innovative work to assembling, advertising, and dissemination.

In addition, the impact of Johnson and Johnson and Pfizer stretches out to the worldwide stage. Their interests in innovative work have progressed the comprehension of different sicknesses and remedial regions, adding to the more extensive field of clinical and drug information. These commitments further develop medical services results as well as invigorate financial development by encouraging a culture of development.

Notwithstanding their monetary commitments, the two organizations are focused on friendly obligation and magnanimity. Johnson and Johnson's humanitarian drives incorporate help for maternal and youngster wellbeing, worldwide wellbeing value, and catastrophe aid ventures. The organization's gifts of clinical supplies and monetary help with reaction to cataclysmic events and worldwide wellbeing emergencies have been instrumental in supporting impacted networks.

Pfizer's charitable endeavors are in basically the same manner expansive, with an emphasis on working on worldwide wellbeing and expanding admittance to medical care for underserved populaces. The organization's help for sickness counteraction and medical services training essentially affects general wellbeing results and has assisted the worldwide wellbeing plan.

The accomplishments and commitments of Johnson and Johnson and Pfizer have been instrumental in propelling general wellbeing and clinical information. Their obligation to patient consideration, exploration, and social obligation has made them worldwide medical care forces to be reckoned with that assume a pivotal part in further developing medical care results and propelling the prosperity of people and networks around the world.

6.1 Analysis of India's pharmaceutical industry and key players.

India's drug industry has arisen as a worldwide force to be reckoned with, eminent for its immense and different assembling capacities, financially savvy drug creation, and imaginative innovative work. In this examination, we will investigate the elements that have pushed India's drug area to global recognition and analyze a portion of the central participants in this powerful industry.

Verifiable Point of view:

India's excursion in the drug business traces all the way back to the mid twentieth hundred years, with the foundation of the primary Indian drug organization in 1901. Nonetheless, it was after India acquired autonomy in 1947 that the business started to prosper. The public authority's attention on confidence and the advancement of native businesses prompted the development of the drug area. The Licenses Demonstration of 1970, which permitted the figuring out of unfamiliar medications, assumed a crucial part in forming the business' scene. This act added to the development of a lively nonexclusive drug industry, which was instrumental in giving reasonable medications to both the Indian populace and the worldwide market.

Key Elements Driving India's Drug Industry:

A few key variables have added to the achievement and development of India's drug industry:

Talented Labor force: India has a huge pool of profoundly gifted researchers, specialists, and drug experts. The accessibility of a skilled labor force has been basic to the business' innovative work capacities.

Savvy Assembling: India's drug industry is known for its practical assembling processes. This benefit is because of variables, for example, lower work expenses, framework, and a deep rooted conventional medication creation framework.

Solid Nonexclusive Medication Assembling: The capacity to deliver great conventional medications has been a foundation of India's drug industry. The nation has earned respect for delivering reasonable, great conventional drugs that act as fundamental medicines for different illnesses.

Vigorous Innovative work: India's drug organizations have put fundamentally in innovative work (Research and development) endeavors. They have teamed up with both homegrown and global exploration associations to foster creative medications and nonexclusive forms of existing drugs.

Various Item Portfolio: India's drug industry delivers a great many drug items, including dynamic drug fixings (APIs), plans, biosimilars, and immunizations. This variety has permitted the business to take care of a worldwide market.

Administrative Consistence: The drug area in India is managed by the Focal Medications Standard Control Association (CDSCO). The adherence to global quality guidelines and administrative necessities has guaranteed the security and adequacy of Indian drug items.

Vital participants in India's Drug Industry:

India's drug industry is home to a few unmistakable players, each making huge commitments to the area. Here are a few critical organizations in the Indian drug scene:

1. **Sun Drug Businesses Restricted:**
   Sun Pharma is perhaps of India's biggest drug organization and one of the top conventional medication producers on the planet. It has major areas of strength for an on Research and development and produces many drug items. Sun Pharma's worldwide presence remembers auxiliaries and tasks for different nations, making it a main player in the business.

2. **Dr. Reddy's Labs:**
   Dr. Reddy's is known for its imaginative innovative work endeavors. It has serious areas of strength for an in the worldwide drug market, offering a different scope of conventional and marked drugs. The organization's joint efforts and acquisitions have extended its item portfolio and reach.

3. **Cipla Restricted:**
   Cipla is a noticeable name in the Indian drug industry, with a solid presence in both homegrown and global business sectors. The organization is prestigious for its commitments to reasonable medical services through the creation of great conventional medications.

4. **Lupin Restricted:**
   Lupin is an exploration driven drug organization with an emphasis on development and the improvement of novel medications. It has a critical worldwide presence and is known for its extensive variety of nonexclusive and specialty drug items.

5. **Aurobindo Pharma:**
   Aurobindo Pharma is a central participant in the worldwide nonexclusive medication market. The organization's obligation to quality and moderateness has pursued it a favored decision

for different medical care establishments and patients around the world.

6. **Biocon Restricted:**

Biocon is a trailblazer in the biotechnology and biosimilars fragment. It has earned worldwide respect for its innovative work of biopharmaceuticals, making it a pivotal player in the worldwide biotech industry.

7. **Zydus Cadila:**

Zydus Cadila is known for its different portfolio, including drugs, biotechnology, and medical care items. The organization's obligation to research and advancement has prompted the improvement of novel medications and medicines.

8. **Glenmark Drugs:**

Glenmark Drugs is an exploration centered drug organization with a worldwide presence. The organization's endeavors in Research and development have prompted the disclosure of imaginative medicines in regions like dermatology, respiratory, and oncology.

9. **Divi's Research facilities:**

Divi's Research facilities is a main maker of APIs and intermediates. The organization's cutting edge producing offices and obligation to quality have situated it as a basic provider of drug fixings to the worldwide business.

10. **Deluge Drugs:**

Deluge Drugs has major areas of strength for an in the Indian drug market. The organization centers around innovative work and delivers a large number of conventional and marked drugs, including cardiovascular and focal sensory system prescriptions.

These central participants in India's drug industry have made significant commitments to medical services advancement, drug producing, and reasonable medical care arrangements. Their obligation to quality, advancement, and administrative consistence has situated them as pioneers in the worldwide drug scene.

Difficulties and Amazing open doors:

While India's drug industry has made momentous progress, it faces a few difficulties and open doors:

Challenges:

Protected innovation Privileges (IPR): The business' dependence on nonexclusive medication creation has prompted worries about protected innovation freedoms and patent-related issues, especially in the worldwide market.

Administrative Consistence: Keeping up with rigid administrative consistence and lining up with global quality principles is difficult for Indian drug organizations.

Value Controls: Government-forced cost controls on drug items in India can affect net revenues for homegrown makers.

Rising Creation Expenses: Factors, for example, expanding work and natural substance expenses can influence the seriousness of Indian drug organizations in the worldwide market.

Quality Confirmation: Guaranteeing steady quality across a different scope of drug items is a continuous test.

Amazing open doors:

Innovative work: Proceeded with interests in Research and development and advancement can prompt the disclosure of novel medications and medicines, growing the item portfolio.

Biosimilars: The turn of events and creation of biosimilars offer critical learning experiences, particularly in the biopharmaceutical area.

Worldwide Associations: Coordinated efforts with global drug organizations can give admittance to new business sectors and innovations.

Medical services Access: The interest for reasonable medical services arrangements, particularly in developing business sectors, presents critical development possibilities.

Computerized Wellbeing: The mix of advanced wellbeing innovations and telemedicine can open up new roads for medical services conveyance and drug deals.

All in all, India's drug industry has accomplished worldwide acknowledgment and praise, driven by a promise to development, reasonable medical care arrangements, and a huge pool of talented experts. Central participants in the business have made critical commitments to medical services advancement, drug assembling, and medical care access.

While the area faces difficulties connected with protected innovation, administrative consistence, and creation costs, it likewise holds huge open doors for development, especially in innovative work, biosimilars, and worldwide associations. The business' strength and flexibility position it as a basic player in the worldwide medical services scene, with the possibility to keep making significant commitments to general wellbeing and prosperity.

6.2 Contributions to global healthcare and accessibility.

The drug and medical care enterprises assume an essential part in working on worldwide wellbeing and openness to clinical therapies. In this extensive examination, we will investigate the commitments these businesses make towards upgrading medical services around the world, guaranteeing admittance to fundamental prescriptions, and tending to worldwide wellbeing challenges.

Worldwide Wellbeing Difficulties:

Prior to digging into the commitments of the drug and medical services enterprises, it's fundamental to comprehend the squeezing worldwide wellbeing challenges that the world countenances. These provokes range from irresistible sicknesses to non-transmittable infections (NCDs), medical care abberations, and arising dangers:

Irresistible Sicknesses: Irresistible illnesses like HIV/Helps, tuberculosis, jungle fever, and arising dangers like Coronavirus keep on presenting huge worldwide wellbeing challenges. These illnesses excessively influence weak populaces in low-and center pay nations.

Non-Transmittable Sicknesses (NCDs): NCDs, including cardio-vascular infections, diabetes, malignant growth, and persistent respiratory illnesses, have become driving reasons for death around the world. NCDs put an impressive weight on medical services frameworks and are frequently connected with way of life factors.

Admittance to Medications: Admittance to fundamental drugs and medical services administrations is a basic worldwide wellbeing challenge. Abberations in access exist both inside and between nations, with many individuals unfit to bear or access life-saving drugs.

Medical care Abberations: Medical care variations in light of elements like pay, orientation, topography, and nationality endure in many areas of the planet. These differences can prompt inconsistent admittance to quality medical care.

Wellbeing Framework Reinforcing: Numerous medical services frameworks, especially in low-and center pay nations, expect fortifying to give compelling and thorough consideration. This incorporates further developing foundation, medical services labor force, and medical services conveyance frameworks.

Commitments to Worldwide Wellbeing and Availability: The drug and medical services ventures are focal in tending to these worldwide wellbeing challenges and further developing medical care access. Their commitments are complex, incorporating different regions:

1. **Innovative work:**

    The drug business assumes a crucial part in drug disclosure and improvement. Its obligation to development has prompted the production of novel drugs, immunizations, and medicines for many infections. These developments are basic in tending to worldwide wellbeing challenges.

    HIV/Helps: The advancement of antiretroviral treatment (Workmanship) has changed the treatment of HIV/Helps. Drug organizations have made huge interests in creating powerful and more reasonable HIV/Helps meds, empowering a large number of individuals to carry on with better existences.

Tuberculosis: New medications and treatment regimens have been created to battle drug-safe tuberculosis. These advancements offer more successful and less harmful treatment choices, especially for multidrug-safe tuberculosis.

Jungle fever: The revelation and advancement of antimalarial medications and insect spray treated bed nets have added to the battle against intestinal sickness. Drug organizations have been engaged with exploring and delivering these life-saving intercessions.

Coronavirus: The quick improvement of Coronavirus immunizations, including mRNA antibodies, has been a demonstration of the drug business' capacity to answer worldwide wellbeing crises. The cooperation between drug organizations, research establishments, and states has sped up antibody advancement and circulation.

NCDs: Innovative work endeavors in the drug business have prompted the production of meds for overseeing NCDs. These meds assist people with conditions like diabetes, hypertension, and cardiovascular sicknesses have better existences.

2. **Nonexclusive Medication Creation:**

India's drug industry, specifically, has been a vital participant in creating reasonable conventional prescriptions. Nonexclusive medications are fundamental in guaranteeing admittance to medicines for different sicknesses, including irresistible illnesses, NCDs, and uncommon circumstances. These reasonable options make it feasible for patients overall to get to fundamental drugs without monetary weight.

3. **Antibodies:**

The turn of events and creation of antibodies are fundamental to infection counteraction and worldwide wellbeing. The drug business, as a team with research establishments and states, has been instrumental in making immunizations that safeguard people and networks from irresistible sicknesses.

Polio: The advancement of the oral polio immunization and its far and wide use has carried the world nearer to annihilating polio. Drug organizations have been imperative in creating and appropriating these immunizations.

Routine Vaccinations: Drug organizations assume a urgent part in the creation of antibodies for routine vaccinations, forestalling illnesses like measles, mumps, rubella, and that's just the beginning.

Crisis Antibodies: During sickness episodes and pandemics, drug organizations work perseveringly to foster immunizations and therapies to battle the spread of irresistible illnesses. This was clear in the fast advancement of Coronavirus immunizations.

4. **Medical care Conveyance and Framework:**
   The drug and medical care enterprises add to further developing medical care conveyance and framework in different ways:

   Medical services Offices: The medical services industry puts resources into the development and the executives of medical clinics, facilities, and clinical focuses. These offices upgrade admittance to medical care administrations, diagnostics, and therapies.

   Telemedicine: The joining of innovation and telemedicine arrangements has further developed admittance to medical services, especially in remote and underserved regions. Telemedicine stages associate patients with medical care experts and give clinical interviews and guidance.

   Store network The board: Drug organizations and medical care suppliers cooperate to guarantee effective inventory network the executives. This incorporates the dissemination of prescriptions, antibodies, and clinical hardware to medical care offices all over the planet.

5. **Public-Private Organizations:**
   Joint effort between people in general and confidential areas

is fundamental in tending to worldwide wellbeing challenges. Public-private associations include state run administrations, drug organizations, non-legislative associations (NGOs), and worldwide associations cooperating to create and execute medical care arrangements.

Antibody Access: Drives like Gavi, the Immunization Union, unite drug organizations, legislatures, and worldwide associations to guarantee fair admittance to immunizations for youngsters in low-pay nations.

Ignored Tropical Infections: Public-private associations target dismissed tropical illnesses (NTDs) by giving free or minimal expense prescriptions to impacted populaces. Drug organizations frequently give these meds to help NTD control and end programs.

6. **Magnanimity and Social Obligation:**

   Drug organizations and medical care associations frequently participate in generous endeavors to help worldwide wellbeing and admittance to medical care. These drives can include monetary gifts, the arrangement of free meds, and backing for medical services foundation.

   Medical care Access Projects: Organizations, for example, Novartis and GlaxoSmithKline have laid out drives to build admittance to drugs for sicknesses like jungle fever and HIV in low-pay nations.

   Clinical Gifts: Giving drugs and clinical supplies to underserved districts during crises, catastrophic events, or infection episodes is a typical charitable activity by drug organizations.

7. **Medical care Preparing and Limit Building:**

Drug and medical care associations frequently put resources into preparing projects and limit working in medical services. This reinforces medical care frameworks, especially in locales with restricted admittance to clinical schooling and preparing.

Clinical Experts: Associations like the Bill and Melinda Doors Establishment support preparing programs for medical services laborers to upgrade their abilities and information, guaranteeing better medical care conveyance.

Neighborhood Assembling: Limit building drives might remember preparing nearby experts for the development of fundamental prescriptions, immunizations, and clinical hardware, lessening dependence on imports.

Difficulties and Potential open doors in Working on Worldwide Medical care and Availability:

While critical headway has been made in working on worldwide medical care and availability, difficulties and valuable open doors continue:

Challenges:

Medical care Variations: Medical services abberations in view of pay, geology, orientation, and nationality keep on restricting admittance to quality medical care in many areas of the planet.

Wellbeing Framework: Deficient medical care foundation, especially in low-pay nations, upsets admittance to quality medical care administrations.

Worldwide Wellbeing Crises: The world should be ready to answer worldwide wellbeing crises, as proven by the Coronavirus pandemic. Guaranteeing evenhanded admittance to medicines and immunizations during crises is a test.

Protected innovation Freedoms (IPR): Protected innovation privileges and patent-related issues can affect admittance to fundamental drugs. Adjusting the requirement for development with reasonable access stays a test.

6.3 Focus on companies like Sun Pharmaceutical and Dr. Reddy's Laboratories.

In the huge scene of India's drug industry, scarcely any organizations stand apart as unmistakably as Sun Drug Businesses and Dr. Reddy's Research facilities. These organizations have made significant commitments to the drug area, both in India and on the worldwide stage. In this examination, we will zero in on Sun Drug Businesses and Dr. Reddy's Research centers, analyzing their set of experiences, key achievements, and their parts in molding the drug scene.

Sun Drug Ventures:

Sun Drug Ventures, ordinarily known as Sun Pharma, is one of India's biggest and most powerful drug organizations. Laid out in 1983 by Dilip Shanghvi, it has developed to turn into a worldwide fore-runner in the business, driven by a guarantee to advancement, quality, and reasonableness.

History and Development:

Sun Pharma's process started with the vision of Dilip Shanghvi, who began the organization with only five items and a modest bunch of representatives. Throughout the long term, the organization extended through a progression of vital acquisitions, coordinated efforts, and natural development. Today, Sun Pharma works in more than 150 nations and has a different item portfolio that incorporates solution and non-prescription drugs, dynamic drug fixings (APIs), and specialty drugs.

Sun Pharma's securing of Ranbaxy Labs in 2014 denoted a huge achievement, hardening its situation as one of the world's biggest nonexclusive drug organizations. This consolidation empowered Sun Pharma to use Ranbaxy's worldwide presence and broad item portfolio, further fortifying its impression in the drug market.

Innovative work (Research and development):

Sun Pharma puts serious areas of strength for an on innovative work, with a guarantee to creating inventive and practical drugs. The organization's Research and development endeavors length many helpful regions, including cardiology, dermatology, psychiatry, nervous system science, and oncology.

One remarkable accomplishment in Sun Pharma's Research and development drives is the improvement of the medication Tildrakizumab, an imaginative treatment for moderate-to-extreme plaque psoriasis. This medication got endorsement from the US Food and Medication

Organization (FDA) in 2018, featuring the organization's devotion to tending to neglected clinical necessities and working on understanding results.

Worldwide Presence:

Sun Pharma's worldwide impression is a demonstration of its obligation to making quality medical care open around the world. The organization's auxiliaries and showcasing arms work in North America, Europe, Latin America, Africa, the Center East, Russia, and the Asia-Pacific locale.

This broad worldwide organization empowers Sun Pharma to give an extensive variety of medical services arrangements, including non-exclusive and marked prescriptions.

Quality Confirmation and Consistence:

Quality and consistence are of most extreme significance to Sun Pharma. The organization's assembling offices stick to severe world-wide quality norms, guaranteeing the security and adequacy of its items. Sun Pharma's obligation to quality and consistence has been perceived through different confirmations, including endorsements from the FDA, European Meds Office (EMA), and the World Wellbeing Association (WHO).

Charitable Endeavors:

Sun Pharma is effectively engaged with different magnanimous drives pointed toward further developing medical services access and local area prosperity. The organization's endeavors incorporate giving clinical consideration to underserved populaces, supporting medical services foundation, and advancing wellbeing training. These drives line up with Sun Pharma's obligation to having a beneficial outcome on society.

Dr. Reddy's Research centers:

Dr. Reddy's Research centers, established by Dr. Anji Reddy in 1984, is one more noticeable player in India's drug industry. The organization has made huge commitments to the advancement of non-exclusive prescriptions, biosimilars, and inventive drugs.

History and Development:

Dr. Reddy's Research centers has a rich history of development and business venture. The organization's initial years were set apart by the creation of dynamic drug fixings (APIs), trailed by the advancement of nonexclusive prescriptions. After some time, Dr. Reddy's extended its range to worldwide business sectors, including the US and Europe, turning into a worldwide drug player.

The organization's organizer, Dr. Anji Reddy, was a visionary chief who had faith in the force of development and examination. His commitment to giving reasonable medical care arrangements established the groundwork for Dr. Reddy's Labs' main goal to work on quiet admittance to quality prescriptions.

Innovative work (Research and development):

Dr. Reddy's Labs has areas of strength for a to innovative work, which has prompted the production of novel medications and biosimilars. The organization's Research and development endeavors center around different remedial regions, including oncology, nervous system science, cardiovascular illnesses, gastroenterology, and dermatology.

One of Dr. Reddy's prominent accomplishments is the advancement of biosimilars, which are biologic prescriptions that are profoundly like existing biologics. Biosimilars offer more reasonable options in contrast to costly biologic medications, extending admittance to basic medicines.

Biosimilars: Dr. Reddy's Research centers created biosimilars for drugs like filgrastim, rituximab, and trastuzumab, which are utilized to treat conditions like malignant growth and immune system illnesses. These biosimilars have been instrumental in making fundamental medicines more available and reasonable for patients.

Worldwide Presence:

Dr. Reddy's Research facilities has a huge worldwide presence with tasks in more than 25 nations. The organization's auxiliaries and partnerships range North America, Europe, Latin America, Russia, and the Asia-Pacific locale. This worldwide reach permits Dr. Reddy's to offer a different scope of drug items to address medical services issues around the world.

Quality Affirmation and Consistence:

Guaranteeing quality and consistence is a main concern for Dr. Reddy's Research facilities. The organization's assembling offices stick to severe worldwide quality norms, acquiring endorsements and affirmations from administrative specialists like the FDA, EMA, and WHO. These certificates verify the organization's obligation to creating protected and viable drugs.

Altruistic Endeavors:

Dr. Reddy's Labs is effectively participated in different altruistic drives that plan to further develop medical care access, schooling, and local area prosperity. The organization's social obligation endeavors incorporate supporting medical care foundation, giving clinical consideration to underserved populaces, and advancing wellbeing and training.

Commitments to Worldwide Medical services and Availability:

Both Sun Drug Enterprises and Dr. Reddy's Labs have made significant commitments to worldwide medical care and openness:

Reasonable Drugs: The development of reasonable conventional prescriptions by these organizations has altogether further developed medical services access for patients around the world. Nonexclusive medications offer financially savvy choices to mark name prescriptions, making medicines more reasonable.

Creative Meds: The advancement of imaginative medications and biosimilars by Sun Pharma and Dr. Reddy's Research facilities has tended to neglected clinical necessities, especially in regions like oncology, immune system sicknesses, and neurological problems.

Worldwide Come to: The broad worldwide presence of these organizations guarantees that medical services arrangements, including meds and immunizations, are open to a different scope of populaces across various mainlands.

Innovative work: The obligation to innovative work has prompted the production of novel prescriptions and biosimilars, working on the nature of medical services for patients with different ailments.

Quality and Consistence: The two organizations stick to rigid quality and consistence guidelines, guaranteeing that their items meet security and viability necessities. This obligation to quality straightforwardly affects the prosperity of patients.

Charitable Drives: Sun Pharma and Dr. Reddy's Research facilities take part in generous exercises pointed toward further developing medical care framework, local area prosperity, and medical services access. These drives support underserved populaces and add to cultural government assistance.

Difficulties and Open doors:

While Sun Drug Businesses and Dr. Reddy's Research facilities have made critical commitments to worldwide medical services and openness, difficulties and amazing open doors endure:

Challenges:

Protected innovation Privileges (IPR): The drug business faces difficulties connected with protected innovation freedoms and patent-related issues, which can influence admittance to fundamental meds.

Medical care Abberations: Variations in admittance to quality medical care endure all around the world, with weak populaces confronting hindrances to clinical therapies.

Worldwide Wellbeing Crises: Planning for and answering worldwide wellbeing crises, as shown by the Coronavirus pandemic, stays a test in guaranteeing evenhanded admittance to medicines and immunizations.

Administrative Consistence: Sticking to severe worldwide administrative norms and quality necessities keeps on being difficult for drug organizations.

Potential open doors:

Innovative work: Proceeded with interests in innovative work offer chances to find novel prescriptions and creative answers for address worldwide wellbeing challenges.

Worldwide Coordinated effort: Coordinated efforts between legislatures, drug organizations, non-administrative associations, and global associations present open doors for additional powerful reactions to worldwide wellbeing challenges.

Advanced Wellbeing: The joining of computerized wellbeing innovations, telemedicine, and medical care data frameworks offers valuable chances to improve medical services conveyance and openness.

Chapter 7

The Automotive Sector

The car area has gone through an exceptional change over the course of the last 100 years. From its modest starting points in the late nineteenth hundred years to the current day, the business has seen huge headways in innovation, plan, and worldwide reach. This paper investigates the vital achievements and difficulties looked by the car area, featuring its development and its suggestions for society, the climate, and the worldwide economy.

In the mid twentieth 100 years, the car area was in its earliest stages. The creation of the car, frequently credited to Karl Benz and his Benz Patent-Motorwagen in 1886, denoted the introduction of another period in transportation. These early vehicles were to a great extent costly and saved for the tip top. Notwithstanding, as innovation progressed and large scale manufacturing methods were presented, the business went through a huge change.

Henry Passage's presentation of the sequential construction system in 1913 upset vehicle creation. This advancement diminished the expense of assembling and made vehicles more reasonable for the overall population. The Portage Model T, frequently alluded to as the

"Dilapidated car," turned into an image of large scale manufacturing and openness. It was a significant crossroads throughout the entire existence of the auto area, democratizing versatility and preparing for far and wide auto possession.

The auto area's development and change were additionally profoundly entwined with financial and social changes. The 1920s denoted a time of success in the US, and the car turned into an image of the Pursuit of happiness. Suburbanization turned into a characterizing pattern, as individuals created some distance from packed metropolitan habitats and into recently constructed networks, worked with by the opportunity and comfort that cars advertised. This change in way of life had broad outcomes, remembering changes for city arranging, the ascent of the cheap food industry, and the improvement of side of the road attractions and inns.

The auto area's worldwide development picked up speed during the mid-twentieth hundred years. American automakers like General Engines, Portage, and Chrysler became commonly recognized names. They assumed a urgent part in the improvement of the auto area overall through their assembling and showcasing systems. The idea of arranged out of date quality, in which vehicles were purposefully intended to have a restricted life expectancy, prodded buyer interest for new vehicles and drove deals.

The car area additionally experienced huge innovative progressions during this period. The 1950s and 1960s saw the improvement of security highlights like safety belts and fold zones, pointed toward decreasing the seriousness of mishaps. Developments in motor innovation and eco-friendliness worked on the natural effect of vehicles. These turns of events, combined with expanded regard for plan and style, prompted the expansion of the auto market, with a developing accentuation on customer inclinations.

The 1970s achieved another arrangement of difficulties for the car area. The oil emergency of 1973 uncovered the business' weakness to variances in energy costs. Buyers and policymakers started to request more eco-friendly vehicles. As a reaction to these worries, the business began to zero in on innovative work in regions like mixture and electric vehicle innovation.

While the 1980s and 1990s were set apart by globalization and the rise of unfamiliar automakers in the US and different business sectors, homegrown organizations confronted expanded contest. Japanese makers like Toyota and Honda acquired a standing for delivering dependable and eco-friendly vehicles. In the interim, European automakers like Volkswagen and BMW took care of buyers looking for extravagance and execution.

The car area kept on advancing in the 21st hundred years, as supportability and natural worries came to the front. Environmental change, air contamination, and reliance on petroleum products prompted a push for cleaner and more feasible transportation choices. Electric vehicles (EVs) acquired fame, with organizations like Tesla spearheading the turn of events and commercialization of every electric vehicle. State run administrations all over the planet acquainted motivators and guidelines with advance EV reception and lessen fossil fuel byproducts.

Notwithstanding EVs, the auto area embraced different advancements like independent driving innovation and associated vehicles. These advancements can possibly rethink the manner in which we ponder transportation. Independent vehicles, specifically, can possibly further develop street security, diminish gridlock, and give portability answers for individuals who can't drive because old enough, incapacity, or different elements.

The car area's change goes past mechanical progressions. It likewise reflects changing purchaser inclinations and a developing consciousness of the natural effect of transportation. Individuals are progressively searching for greener and more manageable choices. Vehicle sharing and ride-hailing administrations, as Uber and Lyft, have acquired fame in metropolitan regions, decreasing the requirement for individual vehicle proprietorship and advancing a more effective utilization of transportation assets.

The shift toward maintainability has additionally prompted the improvement of elective fuel sources, for example, hydrogen energy components and biofuels. These advancements offer the possibility to lessen ozone harming substance discharges and abatement the area's dependence on non-renewable energy sources. Besides, producers are investigating the utilization of lightweight materials and high level assembling methods to further develop eco-friendliness and diminish the natural impression of vehicles.

The car area's effect on society reaches out past the actual items. It assumes an imperative part in the worldwide economy, giving huge number of occupations and contributing essentially to Gross domestic product in numerous nations. The business' production network includes an intricate organization of providers, makers, showrooms, and specialist co-ops, supporting different nearby economies. The car area's financial impact reaches out past its nearby members, influencing areas like steel, elastic, and hardware.

The car area likewise stands firm on an extraordinary footing in worldwide exchange. It has for quite some time been a foundation of worldwide exchange, with vehicles, parts, and parts being sent out and imported for a gigantic scope. The business' worldwide nature implies that disturbances in a single region of the planet can have expansive ramifications for makers, providers, and buyers around the world. For example, the Coronavirus pandemic featured the weakness of the auto store network, as lockdowns and limitations upset creation and prompted deficiencies of key parts.

Besides, the auto area is intently attached to government arrangements and guidelines. Emanations principles, security necessities, and economic deals all significantly affect the business' tasks. Legislatures overall are progressively pushing for stricter outflows guidelines to battle environmental change. This has prompted a race among automakers to foster all the more harmless to the ecosystem vehicles, whether through zap, hydrogen, or different means. Impetuses and endowments for EVs have become normal apparatuses to empower their reception.

The car area's relationship with government strategy isn't restricted to natural worries. It likewise incorporates issues connected with security and purchaser insurance. Guidelines, for example, crash testing, airbag necessities, and vehicle reviews are fundamental for guaranteeing the wellbeing of vehicles out and about. Furthermore, the business is intensely impacted in terms of professional career strategies and taxes, as cross-line exchange stays an essential part of the worldwide auto store network.

One of the business' persevering through difficulties is guaranteeing the wellbeing of vehicles and street clients. Notwithstanding various advances in innovation, engine vehicle mishaps stay a main source of injury and passing around the world. The car area has gained impressive headway in creating wellbeing highlights like non-freezing stopping devices, airbags, electronic soundness control, and high level driver help frameworks (ADAS). Be that as it may, the presentation of independent vehicles and the mix of man-made intelligence and AI into the driving experience bring up issues about security, risk, and morals.

Independent vehicles, while promising better street wellbeing, likewise present difficulties connected with their unwavering quality, online protection, and the requirement for strong guidelines. Guaranteeing that these vehicles can work securely in a blended climate in with customary, human-driven vehicles is a perplexing undertaking. Moreover, worries about information security and the potential for hacking and vindictive exercises in an associated and independent vehicle scene should be tended to.

The auto area's change likewise has suggestions for business. The computerization of assembling processes and the advancement of independent vehicles might prompt changes in the labor force, possibly lessening the interest for particular kinds of positions while setting out new open doors in fields like programming improvement, information examination, and online protection. The shift to electric vehicles may likewise have ramifications for the oil and gas industry, affecting position in extraction, refining, and appropriation.

One more significant part of the car area's advancement is its effect on the climate. The area has generally been a critical supporter of air contamination and ozone depleting substance discharges. The extraction and handling of non-renewable energy sources, as well as the emanations from gas powered motor vehicles, have raised worries about their natural effect. To resolve these issues, states and industry players have attempted to foster cleaner and more manageable transportation arrangements.

7.1 Spotlight on India's automotive industry, with a focus on Tata Motors and Mahindra & Mahindra.

India's auto industry has arisen as a central participant on the world-wide stage, making critical commitments to the country's financial development and mechanical turn of events. This exposition focuses on India's car area, with a particular spotlight on two conspicuous organizations, Goodbye Engines and Mahindra and Mahindra.

The Indian auto industry has encountered exceptional development and change in ongoing many years. While the business' starting points can be followed back to the mid twentieth hundred years, it was only after the post-advancement period during the 1990s that the area really started to take off. With the progression of the Indian economy in 1991, the car business encountered a flood in unfamiliar ventures, mechanical headways, and the section of global players into the Indian market.

Goodbye Engines, an auxiliary of the Goodbye Gathering, has been a critical player in this excursion. Laid out in 1945, Goodbye Engines is presently one of India's biggest and most notable car organizations. The organization has a different item portfolio, including traveler vehicles, business vehicles, and guard vehicles, and is perceived for its develop-ment and obligation to natural manageability.

Mahindra and Mahindra, frequently alluded to as Mahindra, is one more auto monster in India. Established in 1945, it has developed into a worldwide combination with an emphasis on areas like car, avia-tion, and agribusiness. Mahindra has become well known in the auto business with many items, including utility vehicles, farm haulers, and electric vehicles.

Both Goodbye Engines and Mahindra and Mahindra play played crucial parts in molding the Indian car industry, and their accounts merit investigating exhaustively.

Goodbye Engines, under the initiative of the Goodbye Gathering, has been a vital driver of India's car area. The organization's set of experiences is set apart by a few achievements that have added to its development and achievement. One of the main accomplishments in Goodbye Engines' set of experiences is the turn of events and send off of the Goodbye Indica in 1998. This was India's most memorable traveler vehicle planned, created, and fabricated altogether in-house. The Indica's prosperity denoted a defining moment in the Indian car industry, showing the way that Indian organizations could rival world-wide players concerning configuration, designing, and quality.

Goodbye Engines proceeded to advance and extend its item range with the send off of the Goodbye Nano in 2008. Promoted as the world's least expensive vehicle, the Nano planned to make vehicle pos-session more available to the Indian populace. While the Nano earned consideration for its moderateness and creative plan, it confronted difficulties, including wellbeing concerns and issues connected with its production line's area in Singur, West Bengal. These difficulties featured the intricacies of the Indian car market and the requirement for organi-zations to think about different elements, including wellbeing, quality, and social and ecological effects.

In the business vehicle fragment, Goodbye Engines has been a pre-dominant power. The organization's scope of trucks, transports, and business vehicles has been instrumental in supporting India's coordi-nated operations and transportation industry. Goodbye Engines'

obligation to advancement and supportability is obvious in its im-provement of electric and crossover business vehicles, taking special care of the developing interest for cleaner and more eco-friendly transporta-tion choices.

Goodbye Engines has additionally made huge introductions to the electric vehicle (EV) market with the Goodbye Tigor EV and the Goodbye Nexon EV. As the world progressively centers around lessening fossil fuel byproducts and battling environmental change, Goodbye Engines is situating itself to be a forerunner in the progress to electric portability in India.

Additionally, Goodbye Engines' worldwide development has been important. The procurement of Panther Land Meanderer (JLR) in 2008 denoted a huge achievement in the organization's worldwide impression. This securing not just gave Goodbye Engines admittance to extravagance vehicle marks yet in addition gave chances to cross-fertilization of innovation and ability. JLR's prosperity under Goodbye Engines' possession mirrors the organization's obligation to sustaining and developing procured brands.

Mahindra and Mahindra, then again, has its own account of development and enhancement. The organization's underlying foundations are in the development of agrarian hardware, fundamentally work vehicles. Mahindra's work vehicles have been fundamental in modernizing Indian agribusiness, further developing ranch efficiency, and enabling provincial networks.

Mahindra's enhancement into the car area started with the creation of utility vehicles. The Mahindra Scorpio, sent off in 2002, denoted a huge move toward the organization's venture into traveler vehicles. The Scorpio's prosperity exhibited that Mahindra had the abilities to produce vehicles that could contend with worldwide norms regarding execution and wellbeing.

One of the champion highlights of Mahindra's way to deal with car producing is its emphasis on roughness and rough terrain ability, which has reverberated with purchasers in India and different global business sectors. Models like the Mahindra Thar, Bolero, and XUV500 have become well known options for those looking for vehicles that can deal with testing territories.

Besides, Mahindra has embraced the electric vehicle transformation. The Mahindra e2o, India's most memorable electric vehicle, was sent off in 2013. The organization has since extended its electric vehicle portfolio to incorporate electric vehicles, electric three-wheelers, and electric transports. Mahindra Electric, an auxiliary of Mahindra and Mahindra, is a huge player in the Indian EV market.

The organization's introduction to electric portability lines up with the Indian government's vision of advancing electric vehicles and decreasing the country's reliance on non-renewable energy sources. Subsequently, Mahindra has situated itself as a forerunner in the electric vehicle market, offering a scope of items intended to meet the one of a kind requirements of Indian shoppers.

Mahindra and Mahindra has additionally wandered into the worldwide market with acquisitions and joint endeavors. The securing of SsangYong Engine Organization, a South Korean automaker, in 2011, extended Mahindra's worldwide presence and gave admittance to innovation and designing skill. The organization with Portage in 2019 pointed toward working together on item improvement, conveyance, and jolt additionally set Mahindra's desires in the global car field.

Both Goodbye Engines and Mahindra and Mahindra have confronted their portion of difficulties. The exceptionally cutthroat and cost delicate Indian market expects organizations to ceaselessly develop, work on quality, and adjust to changing shopper inclinations. The two organizations have needed to resolve issues connected with security and natural effect. They have likewise needed to explore complex administrative conditions and exchange arrangements India and universally.

The Indian car industry has gained significant headway as of late. Be that as it may, it faces a few difficulties and valuable open doors. One of the principal challenges is the requirement for cleaner and more practical transportation arrangements. India's quickly developing metropolitan populace and expanding vehicle proprietorship rates have prompted issues like gridlock and air contamination. This has incited a push for electric vehicles, cleaner energizes, and worked on open transportation.

Goodbye Engines and Mahindra and Mahindra have been at the very front of this shift towards maintainability. Goodbye Engines, with its electric vehicle contributions like the Goodbye Nexon EV and the Goodbye Tigor EV, is focused on decreasing the carbon impression of transportation. Mahindra, with its broad scope of electric vehicles, is adding to India's electric portability unrest. The public authority's Quicker Reception and Assembling of Half and half and Electric Vehicles (Notoriety) conspire has given motivating forces to advance the reception of electric vehicles.

The Indian government's "Make in India" crusade, sent off in 2014, is one more drive pointed toward supporting the homegrown assembling area, including the auto business. The mission energizes unfamiliar direct speculation and the improvement of a powerful assembling environment in India. This drive can possibly draw in additional unfamiliar auto organizations to put resources into India and add to the country's financial development.

The Indian car area's globalization has not just carried unfamiliar players into the Indian market however has likewise empowered Indian organizations to universally grow their presence. Goodbye Engines' obtaining of Puma Land Wanderer is a demonstration of India's capacity to contend and prevail in the worldwide auto market. Moreover, Mahindra's acquisitions and organizations have assisted the organization with laying out a worldwide impression.

India's essential area, gifted labor force, and serious assembling costs make it an appealing objective for global car organizations. The country's solid designing and IT areas give an information base to auto innovative work. Besides, India's enormous homegrown market offers amazing open doors for both neighborhood and global players to create and send off new items.

The Indian auto industry is additionally adjusting to changing customer inclinations and innovative progressions. Availability, man-made brainpower, and independent driving innovations are steadily advancing into vehicles. The interest for further developed infotainment frameworks, security elements, and brilliant availability choices has been on the ascent.

The idea of portability as-a-administration (MaaS) is building up forward momentum, with organizations investigating imaginative transportation arrangements past conventional vehicle proprietorship. Ride-sharing administrations, electric bikes, and e-bicycles are turning out to be progressively famous in metropolitan regions. Both Goodbye Engines and Mahindra and Mahindra are adjusting to these patterns by investigating amazing open doors in the common portability space.

7.2 Evolution of the sector and adaptation to changing trends.

The development of businesses and their variation to changing patterns are major perspectives that direct their prosperity and significance in a dynamic and cutthroat world. This paper intends to investigate how different areas have developed over the long run and adjusted to adapt to arising patterns, mechanical headways, and changing purchaser ways of behaving.

Businesses across the range have gone through huge changes driven by mechanical development, financial movements, and cultural changes. The development cycle has been especially striking in areas like the auto business, data innovation, medical services, and retail. These ventures have encountered significant changes in their tasks, items, and administrations to remain pertinent and cutthroat in a quickly evolving scene.

The car area, for example, has persistently adjusted to changing patterns throughout the long term. From its initial days set apart by the development of the auto to the current time of electric and independent vehicles, the business has seen massive mechanical progressions. Makers have presented wellbeing highlights, further developed eco-friendliness, and investigated elective fuel sources because of developing worries about natural effect and supportability.

The coordination of innovation into vehicles has been a critical pattern in the auto area. The improvement of cutting edge driver-help frameworks (ADAS, for example, path keeping help and versatile journey control, has fundamentally upgraded security and accommodation for drivers. Besides, the presentation of electric and crossover vehicles as a reaction to ecological worries and moving shopper inclinations toward cleaner transportation addresses a significant variation in the business.

The auto business' continuous shift towards independent vehicles is another critical pattern. Organizations are putting vigorously in innovative work to carry self-driving vehicles to the market, planning to reform transportation and further develop street wellbeing. The idea of associated and independent vehicles addresses a huge transformation, though one that faces administrative, moral, and mechanical difficulties.

Likewise, the data innovation area has gone through a noteworthy development, portrayed by quick headways in equipment, programming, and the web. The approach of the web and the ensuing advanced transformation have changed the manner in which individuals impart, work, and direct business. The area has adjusted to arising patterns by continually enhancing and growing new innovations to meet the advancing requirements of organizations and shoppers.

Distributed computing, computerized reasoning (simulated intelligence), huge information, and the Web of Things (IoT) are a portion of the conspicuous patterns in the IT business. Distributed computing has upset information capacity and handling, offering adaptability, adaptability, and cost-adequacy. Artificial intelligence and AI have tracked down applications in different spaces, from customized proposals in web based business to prescient examination in medical care and money. The IoT has empowered the interconnectivity of gadgets, prompting savvy homes, wearable innovation, and worked on modern proficiency.

The medical services area has encountered its own arrangement of changes and variations, especially because of mechanical progressions and segment shifts. The combination of innovation in medical services, known as wellbeing tech, has prompted the improvement of telemedicine, electronic wellbeing records, wearable wellbeing checking gadgets, and customized medication. These progressions have intended to upgrade patient consideration, further develop diagnostics, and make medical care more open and effective.

Moreover, the Coronavirus pandemic went about as an impetus for development and transformation in the medical care area. The emergency sped up the reception of telehealth administrations, distant patient observing, and computerized wellbeing arrangements, mirroring a change in how medical care is conveyed. These progressions were important to address the difficulties presented by the pandemic and have now become fundamental pieces of the medical care scene.

The retail business, customarily dependent on actual stores and in-person shopping encounters, has gone through a huge change in light of changing customer ways of behaving and mechanical headways. Web based business has arisen as a significant pattern, reshaping the manner in which purchasers shop and organizations work. Organizations have adjusted by laying out web-based stages, upgrading advanced promoting systems, and further developing strategies to satisfy the needs of online customers.

The reconciliation of man-made consciousness and information examination in the retail area has changed client encounters. Customized proposals, designated publicizing, and prescient examination have become fundamental devices for retailers to in like manner figure out buyer conduct and designer their contributions. Moreover, the use of omnichannel retailing, where on the web and disconnected channels are coordinated consistently, has turned into a fundamental transformation for retailers to give a firm shopping experience.

Adjusting to changing patterns is a perplexing and progressing process for enterprises. It requires a proactive methodology, spryness, and an eagerness to embrace development. Organizations that prevail with regards to adjusting to patterns are in many cases those that put resources into innovative work, encourage a culture of development, and stay receptive to customer needs and market elements.

The way to effective transformation lies in a blend of variables, including mechanical development, statistical surveying, client criticism, and a sharp comprehension of cultural movements. An adaptable and ground breaking approach is important to expect and answer changing patterns successfully.

Notwithstanding, transformation to changing patterns additionally presents difficulties. Businesses frequently face obstacles like administrative limitations, asset imperatives, rivalry, and the requirement for significant interests in new advancements. Exploring these difficulties requires vital preparation, risk the executives, and a readiness to embrace change.

Additionally, businesses should be discerning of the moral ramifications of their variations. As innovation keeps on developing, moral contemplations encompassing information protection, network safety, and the effect on the labor force become progressively significant. Offsetting mechanical headway with moral obligation is essential for economical and dependable industry advancement.

The course of transformation is definitely not a one-time occasion yet a continuous excursion. Ventures should be ready to develop and advance to consistently remain serious and meet the always changing necessities of their buyers. Adaptability, flexibility, and a promise to remaining at the very front of development are fundamental for long haul achievement.

All in all, the development of ventures and their transformation to changing patterns are fundamental parts of their development and supportability. The auto, data innovation, medical services, and retail areas are significant of enterprises that have gone through significant changes because of mechanical headways, cultural moves, and changing buyer ways of behaving.

Adjusting to arising patterns requires a diverse methodology, consolidating development, innovative progressions, statistical surveying, and a profound comprehension of buyer needs. Fruitful transformation requires a continuous obligation to change and an eagerness to embrace new innovations and strategies to fulfill the developing needs of the market.

As businesses proceed to develop and adjust, they should explore difficulties, including administrative limitations, moral contemplations, and the requirement for critical ventures. Embracing development and moral obligation while remaining receptive to changing patterns will be pivotal for businesses to flourish in a quickly changing and cutthroat worldwide scene.

7.3 Influence on the domestic and global automotive market.

The car business holds a novel and vital spot in both the home-grown and worldwide business sectors. The area's impact reaches out a long ways past the creation of vehicles, influencing economies, work markets, transportation foundation, and ecological supportability. This paper dives into the significant impact of the car business on both homegrown and worldwide scales, revealing insight into the financial, social, and ecological elements of its effect.

At the homegrown level, the car business impacts the economy of a country. It is in many cases thought about a financial gauge, mirroring the general wellbeing of the country's economy. The car area adds to the GDP (Gross domestic product) through the creation, deal, and adjusting of vehicles. Besides, it frames a complicated snare of interrelated organizations that envelop producing, providers, showrooms, and administration focuses, creating income and business open doors.

The creation and offer of vehicles straightforwardly affect a nation's economy. It encourages fabricating position and invigorates related businesses like steel, plastics, elastic, gadgets, and different parts. More-over, the car area is an indispensable wellspring of government income through charges on vehicle deals and import obligations. The business' cooperative relationship with different areas of the economy underlines its significance in advancing monetary development and improvement.

The car area's impact on work is especially significant. It extends to an extensive variety of open positions, from assembly line laborers engaged with vehicle gathering to engineers work in innovative work. Past assembling, there are occupations in deals, showcasing, coordinated factors, upkeep, and backing administrations. In the US, for example, the auto business is perhaps of the biggest manager, straightforwardly or in a roundabout way giving position to a great many individuals.

Notwithstanding business, the auto business significantly affects expertise improvement and schooling. It drives the interest for a gifted and different labor force, from specialists and creators to experts and deals experts. Moreover, it prompts interests in specialized and professional schooling projects to guarantee that the labor force is exceptional to meet the business' developing necessities.

The car area is likewise profoundly implanted in the transportation framework of a country. It adds to the turn of events and upkeep of streets, thruways, and extensions, as well as the development of corner stores, support offices, and charging framework for electric vehicles. The business assumes a part in molding metropolitan preparation and framework improvement to oblige the necessities of a steadily developing populace of vehicle proprietors and suburbanites.

Past its financial and framework commitments, the car area has social ramifications. Possessing a vehicle has for quite some time been related with opportunity and portability, empowering people to get to occupations, instruction, and administrations. Be that as it may, it likewise raises worries about metropolitan blockage, traffic wellbeing, and the ecological effect of transportation.

While the car business fills monetary development and makes occupations, it has been wrestling with squeezing natural difficulties. The discharges from gas powered motor vehicles, basically controlled by petroleum derivatives, have been a significant supporter of air contamination and ozone harming substance emanations. These discharges are answerable for different natural issues, including environmental change and general wellbeing concerns.

As a reaction to these difficulties, the business has started a change in outlook towards greener and more maintainable transportation arrangements. The turn of events and creation of electric vehicles (EVs) is one of the main variations to address natural worries. EVs produce zero tailpipe outflows, lessening air contamination and reliance on non-renewable energy sources. States all over the planet have presented motivating forces, endowments, and guidelines to energize the reception of EVs and decrease fossil fuel byproducts.

The impact of the car area expands all around the world, forming the elements of global exchange, tact, and mechanical development. The area's effect on the worldwide stage is multi-layered and underlines the significance of global collaboration, contest, and guideline.

Global exchange assumes a urgent part the auto business. Vehicles, parts, and parts are sent out and imported for an enormous scope, with worldwide stock chains interfacing producers, providers, and buyers around the world. Organizations depend on worldwide exchange to get to unrefined substances, advances, and new business sectors, promoting their worldwide extension. Global economic deals and taxes additionally influence the business' tasks, molding the expense and availability of vehicles in various areas.

The worldwide reach of the auto business is clear through the global presence of central parts like General Engines, Toyota, Volkswagen, and Passage. These global enterprises have creation offices, deals outlets, and exploration focuses in different nations, adding to nearby economies and occupation markets. They likewise participate in worldwide innovative work joint efforts to drive mechanical development.

The auto area's globalization isn't simply restricted to laid out players yet in addition reaches out to developing business sectors. Nations like China and India have seen a flood in car assembling and utilization, mirroring the changing elements of the business. These business sectors offer open doors for development and extension, and worldwide organizations are quick to lay out a presence to take advantage of the huge shopper base.

In the domain of mechanical development, the car business assumes an essential part in forming headways in designing, materials science, and data innovation. The improvement of security highlights, energy-effective motors, and associated vehicle innovation have a sweeping effect, on the auto area as well as on the more extensive innovation scene.

Wellbeing advancements like airbags, non-freezing stopping devices, and electronic dependability control have been created and refined in light of the need to lessen the seriousness of mishaps and further develop street security. These advances have applications past the auto area and have added to the more extensive reception of security highlights in different enterprises.

The journey for energy-proficient motors and decreased outflows has prompted developments in motor innovation, lightweight materials, and elective fuel sources. These improvements have made vehicles more eco-friendly as well as impacted energy strategy, supportable transportation, and emanations guidelines at the public and worldwide levels.

The combination of innovation into vehicles, known as associated vehicles, is one more critical pattern in the auto business. This incorporates highlights like in-vehicle theater setups, GPS route, telematics, and correspondence with different vehicles and foundation. Such headways have worked on the driving experience as well as have expected ramifications for transportation security, traffic the executives, and the advancement of independent vehicles.

The car area's push towards independent vehicles, vehicles equipped for self-driving, addresses a significant innovative jump. Organizations are putting vigorously in innovative work to carry self-driving vehicles to the market, meaning to reform transportation and further develop street security. Independent vehicles can possibly diminish mishaps brought about by human blunder, increment the productivity of traffic the board, and give versatility answers for individuals who can't drive because old enough, inability, or different variables.

The worldwide auto industry is set apart by serious contest and quick mechanical progressions. Organizations are persistently competing to improve, secure licenses, and gain an upper hand. This furious contest has prompted cross-line consolidations, acquisitions, and joint efforts, mirroring the worldwide idea of the business.

The car business' globalization and innovative headways have likewise required worldwide collaboration and guideline. Administrative bodies like the Unified Countries Monetary Commission for Europe (UNECE) have acquainted security and emanations guidelines with guarantee vehicles meet least prerequisites for wellbeing and ecological effect.

These guidelines mean to fit guidelines across various areas, working with worldwide exchange and collaboration.

The business' global presence is additionally reflected in the improvement of electric vehicles. Significant automakers are extending their electric vehicle contributions to take care of the developing worldwide interest for cleaner transportation choices. Also, headways in battery innovation and charging foundation have worldwide ramifications, as electric vehicles rise above public boundaries, requiring global guidelines and participation.

The auto business' worldwide impact is additionally highlighted by its commitment to natural maintainability. As the world wrestles with the difficulties of environmental change and ecological debasement, the area's shift toward electric vehicles, lightweight materials, and manageable assembling rehearses has a significant effect. Electric vehicles, specifically, have acquired noticeable quality as a cleaner option in contrast to customary gas and diesel-fueled vehicles.

Be that as it may, the ecological advantages of electric vehicles really rely on how the power used to charge them is produced. A shift to sustainable power hotspots for power age is fundamental to boost the ecological benefits of electric vehicles. Legislatures and associations are zeroing in on the advancement of economical energy framework to help the development.

8 |

Chapter 8

The Future of India's Industrial Giants

India's modern goliaths play had a focal impact in the country's monetary turn of events and have become compelling players on the worldwide stage. These combinations, with their assorted advantages crossing different areas, have been instrumental in forming India's modern scene. This exposition investigates the eventual fate of India's modern goliaths, zeroing in on a few key combinations, including Goodbye Gathering, Dependence Enterprises, and Aditya Birla Gathering.

The Goodbye Gathering, established in 1868 by Jamsetji Goodbye, is one of India's most established and most esteemed modern aggregates. It has a presence in a large number of enterprises, including steel, vehicles, data innovation, broadcast communications, and buyer products. Throughout the long term, Goodbye Gathering has shown flexibility and versatility, reliably developing to meet the changing requirements of the market.

Looking forward, the Goodbye Gathering's future lies in advancement and manageability. In the auto area, Goodbye Engines, the gathering's lead organization, is taking huge steps in electric vehicles. The Goodbye Nexon EV and the Goodbye Tigor EV are proof of the organization's obligation to eco-accommodating transportation. The auto business is going through a worldwide shift towards electric versatility, and Goodbye Engines is situating itself as a forerunner in this change.

Goodbye Consultancy Administrations (TCS), the IT administrations arm of the Goodbye Gathering, is a worldwide IT benefits and counseling goliath. TCS has a presence in north of 45 nations and serves clients across different ventures. The organization's future development lies in advanced change, man-made consciousness, and information examination. As associations overall hug computerized innovations, TCS is strategically set up to give imaginative arrangements and drive mechanical progressions.

The Goodbye Gathering is likewise effectively taken part in the improvement of reasonable and sustainable power arrangements. Goodbye Power, one of India's biggest coordinated power organizations, is putting resources into environmentally friendly power sources, including wind and sun based power. The organization is focused on decreasing its carbon impression and advancing clean energy age. This lines up with India's aggressive objectives for sustainable power and natural supportability.

Moreover, the Goodbye Gathering has shown a commitment to social obligation through drives, for example, the Goodbye Trusts, which center around training, medical services, and country improvement. These endeavors are characteristic of the gathering's obligation to working on the personal satisfaction for individuals in India and then some.

Dependence Enterprises, under the initiative of Mukesh Ambani, has become perhaps of India's generally noticeable combination. It works in assorted areas, including petrochemicals, broadcast communications, retail, and advanced administrations. Dependence's vision for what's in store rotates around digitization, web based business, and sustainable power.

Dependence Jio, the broadcast communications arm of Dependence Enterprises, has disturbed the Indian telecom market. The organization's emphasis on high velocity web, reasonable information plans, and imaginative advanced administrations has accumulated large number of supporters. The fate of Dependence Jio is supposed to bring 5G availability, Web of Things (IoT) benefits, and further computerized advancements to India.

Dependence Retail, the retail arm of the aggregate, has quickly extended and presently works in different portions, including staple, hardware, and design. With its procurement of Future Gathering, Dependence Retail is ready to turn into the prevailing player in India's retail area. The reconciliation of on the web and disconnected retail, joined with an extensive variety of customer contributions, is supposed to fuel Dependence's development.

Dependence's obligation to sustainable power is obvious through its aggressive plans in the area. The organization expects to be a net-zero carbon producer by 2035. It is putting vigorously in sun based energy, wind power, and green hydrogen creation. As the world movements towards feasible energy sources, Dependence's accentuation on renewables positions it as a central part in India's perfect energy change.

In addition, Dependence Ventures is investigating open doors in the computerized space, including web based business, advanced installments, and cloud administrations. The combination's reconciliation of innovation and purchaser administrations underlines its yearning to be a computerized force to be reckoned with. As India's computerized scene advances, Dependence is strategically set up to benefit from the nation's developing computerized economy.

Aditya Birla Gathering, drove by Kumar Mangalam Birla, is one more huge combination with a different arrangement of organizations, including metals, concrete, materials, media communications, and monetary administrations. The gathering's future rotates around supportability, computerized change, and worldwide development.

Aditya Birla Gathering's concrete business is centered around eco-accommodating development arrangements. The organization means to decrease its carbon impression through feasible works on, including the utilization of elective energizes and energy-effective advancements. As urbanization and framework advancement proceed, the interest for supportable development materials is supposed to rise.

In the monetary administrations area, Aditya Birla Capital is endeavoring to give thorough monetary arrangements, including protection, resource the board, and loaning. As India's working class extends, the interest for monetary administrations is developing. Aditya Birla Gathering is strategically set up to take care of this market, giving a great many monetary items and administrations.

The gathering's broadcast communications arm, Vodafone Thought Restricted, is adjusting to the quickly advancing telecom market in India. With the rollout of 5G innovation, Vodafone Thought intends to give high velocity availability and worked on advanced administrations. As the interest for information and computerized administrations keeps on developing, Vodafone Thought is supposed to assume a critical part in India's telecom industry.

Notwithstanding its homegrown presence, Aditya Birla Gathering is effectively extending its worldwide impression. The obtaining of aluminum producer Aleris positions the gathering as a central member in the worldwide aluminum industry. This worldwide development is demonstrative of the gathering's desire to enhance and access new business sectors.

The fate of India's modern goliaths is likewise entwined with the nation's financial and strategy scene. The Indian government's "Make in India" crusade, sent off in 2014, means to advance homegrown assembling and draw in unfamiliar ventures. It urges organizations to set up creation offices in India, encouraging financial development and occupation creation.

The public authority's "Atmanirbhar Bharat" (Confident India) drive, sent off because of the Coronavirus pandemic, looks to fortify homegrown assembling, decrease reliance on imports, and advance independence. It incorporates motivators and backing for homegrown enterprises, remembering those for the auto, gadgets, and drug areas.

These drives line up with the objectives and yearnings of India's modern goliaths. Organizations like Goodbye Gathering, Dependence Ventures, and Aditya Birla Gathering are effectively putting resources into innovative work, assembling, and development to help these administration drives and add to the country's financial development.

All in all, the eventual fate of India's modern monsters, including Goodbye Gathering, Dependence Enterprises, and Aditya Birla Gathering, is set apart by their obligation to advancement, supportability, and worldwide development. These combinations have shown their versatility and flexibility notwithstanding changing business sector elements and have situated themselves as persuasive players in India's monetary scene.

As they keep on putting resources into state of the art advances, embrace computerized change, and extend their worldwide presence, these modern monsters are driving financial development as well as molding the fate of different areas, from broadcast communications to environmentally friendly power. Their impact isn't restricted to the homegrown market, as they are effectively partaking in India's developing job on the worldwide stage.

The associations and coordinated efforts between these aggregates and the public authority's drives to advance homegrown assembling highlight their necessary job in India's excursion towards confidence and financial flourishing. With their proceeded with obligation to development and supportability, India's modern monsters are exceptional to explore the difficulties and chances representing things to come and assume a crucial part.

8.1 Discussion of the future prospects and challenges facing India's industrial giants.

What's to come prospects and difficulties confronting India's modern monsters, including combinations like Goodbye Gathering,

Dependence Businesses, and Aditya Birla Gathering, are dependent upon a large number of elements, including worldwide financial patterns, mechanical disturbances, administrative changes, and cultural movements. In this conversation, we will dive into the valuable open doors and difficulties that these modern monsters might experience before long.

Future Possibilities

Innovation and Computerized Change: Embracing advanced change is key for India's modern goliaths. As innovation keeps on reshaping enterprises, these combinations have the chance to develop and broaden their plans of action. Digitalization can upgrade functional productivity, further develop client encounters, and make new income streams. For example, Dependence Ventures' introduction to computerized administrations with Jio has reformed India's broadcast communications scene, and its venture into internet business is a demonstration of the potential for advanced disturbance.

Maintainability and Environmentally friendly power: India's modern goliaths have shown a guarantee to supportability, with an emphasis on environmentally friendly power arrangements. The shift toward cleaner energy sources, for example, sun oriented and wind power, offers critical development potential. Goodbye Power and Aditya Birla Gathering, for instance, are effectively putting resources into practical energy age. This lines up with worldwide ecological objectives as well as satisfies the rising need for clean energy sources.

Worldwide Extension and Enhancement: Globalization presents open doors for these combinations to extend their presence in global business sectors. Goodbye Gathering's securing of Puma Land Meanderer and the worldwide development of Aditya Birla Gathering are instances of how Indian modern monsters are looking past their homegrown market. Expansion into new enterprises and areas can likewise lessen hazard and upgrade strength.

Framework and Development: India's aggressive foundation improvement projects, like brilliant urban areas, expressways, and air terminals, offer huge open doors for these modern goliaths. Foundation and development areas are ready for development, and aggregates with interests around there, similar to Aditya Birla Gathering and Goodbye Gathering, can gain by this interest by giving feasible development materials and arrangements.

Social Obligation and Effect Effective financial planning: There is a developing pattern of organizations focusing on friendly obligation. Modern monsters can take advantage of the chance to put resources into drives that emphatically influence society, like schooling, medical care, and provincial turn of events. The Goodbye Trusts' endeavors here mirror the potential for organizations to have a massive effect in the existences of millions of individuals.

Innovative work: Development and examination will assume an essential part later on outcome of these combinations. Goodbye Gathering, for example, has a long history of development and its organization TCS is effectively engaged with state of the art innovations. Innovative work can prompt leap forwards in areas going from medical care to assembling and reinforce the organizations' cutthroat positions.

Coordinated efforts and Associations: Cooperation with different organizations, research establishments, and new companies can open new entryways for development and development. These associations can drive mechanical headways and assist aggregates with remaining in front of the opposition.

Challenges

Worldwide Financial Vulnerability: The worldwide monetary scene is set apart by vulnerabilities, including exchange strains, international contentions, and financial downturns. Such vulnerabilities can affect the development plans and monetary strength of India's modern goliaths. Changes in worldwide exchange arrangements can influence the combinations' capacity to get to worldwide business sectors.

Mechanical Interruption: While innovation presents amazing open doors, it likewise presents difficulties. Fast innovative headways can deliver existing plans of action old. Remaining refreshed and important despite mechanical disturbance is a consistent test, as it requires critical ventures and versatility.

Ecological Guidelines: As the world movements towards natural manageability, stricter ecological guidelines might become an integral factor. Organizations need with comply to these guidelines, which can bring about expanded consistence expenses and influence tasks. The change to cleaner energy sources, while promising, additionally presents difficulties regarding beginning speculations and innovative headways.

Rivalry: The modern scene is profoundly serious. India's modern goliaths contend locally as well as on a worldwide scale. The presence of global companies and new businesses implies that aggregates should persistently advance and remain in front of the opposition.

Political and Administrative Dangers: Political changes and administrative movements can influence business activities. Ventures like broadcast communications, where government strategies and guidelines assume a critical part, are especially helpless to such dangers. An adjustment of administrative position can influence the productivity and development possibilities of combinations.

Production network Disturbances: Ongoing occasions, like the Coronavirus pandemic, have featured the weaknesses in worldwide stock chains. Inventory network disturbances can influence the convenient conveyance of labor and products, prompting income misfortunes and functional difficulties. India's modern monsters need to put resources into strong stockpile chains and hazard the executives systems.

Ability Maintenance and Improvement: Drawing in and holding top ability is a typical test across ventures. To encourage development and adjust to a changing business climate, organizations need a talented labor force. Creating and holding ability is fundamental for supporting development.

Moral and Social Obligation: As organizations face developing investigation for their moral practices, they need to guarantee that their tasks fulfill high moral guidelines. Social and natural obligations are progressively critical, and neglecting to meet them can prompt reputational harm and monetary repercussions.

Network safety: With the rising dependence on advanced innovations, organizations face uplifted network protection chances. Safeguarding touchy information and protecting against digital dangers is a developing concern. A cyberattack can disturb tasks and harm an organization's standing.

Market and Purchaser Patterns: Understanding and adjusting to advancing business sector and buyer patterns is significant. Changing buyer inclinations, like a shift towards manageability and eco-benevolence, can challenge organizations that are delayed to adjust to these patterns.

8.2 Potential for continued growth, innovation, and global impact.

The potential for proceeded with development, advancement, and worldwide effect for India's modern goliaths, including combinations like Goodbye Gathering, Dependence Ventures, and Aditya Birla Gathering, is huge. These associations have shown versatility, flexibility, and a pledge to greatness, situating themselves to outfit the chances representing things to come.

Proceeded with Development:

Venture into Developing Business sectors: India's modern monsters have an amazing chance to grow their impression into developing business sectors. Nations in Africa, Southeast Asia, and South America present undiscovered possibility for development. These areas offer enormous shopper markets and the potential for enhancement of income sources.

Online business and Retail: The Indian web based business area is blasting, and organizations like Dependence Enterprises have perceived the possible in this market. Extending their web based business and retail tasks can essentially add to their development. With the mix of on the web and disconnected retail, these combinations can offer a consistent shopping experience to purchasers.

Producing Center point: India can possibly turn into a worldwide assembling center point, drawing in unfamiliar ventures and working with sends out. As a feature of the "Make in India" crusade, these modern monsters can profit by this drive by reinforcing their assembling capacities and adding to India's monetary development.

Monetary Administrations: India's monetary administrations area offers significant learning experiences. With a rising working class and expanding monetary consideration, organizations like Aditya Birla Gathering can extend their monetary administrations contributions, including protection, resource the board, and loaning.

Shrewd Urban communities and Foundation: India's aggressive brilliant city activities and framework advancement are amazing open doors for development. These combinations can give economical development materials and answers for help these tasks. The development and framework areas are ready for huge extension.

Sustainable power: The shift towards sustainable power sources is a worldwide pattern that presents huge development potential. Goodbye Power and different organizations inside the combinations have the valuable chance to extend their environmentally friendly power tasks, benefiting from the rising interest for clean energy arrangements.

Advancement and Research and development: Proceeded with interest in innovative work (Research and development) and advancement is fundamental for future development. These modern goliaths ought to zero in on creating state of the art advances, items, and administrations that can meet developing business sector needs and drive development.

Development:

Advanced Change: It is basic to Embrace computerized change. Organizations like Goodbye Gathering, Dependence Enterprises, and Aditya Birla Gathering have previously made progress around here, yet the potential for advancement is huge. Further digitization can upgrade functional proficiency and open new roads for administration conveyance and client commitment.

IoT and Network: The Web of Things (IoT) is a developing field with applications in different businesses, from farming to medical services. Advancements in IoT can prompt savvy horticulture, telemedicine, from there, the sky is the limit. Goodbye Consultancy Administrations and Dependence Jio are strategically situated to drive IoT advancements.

Green Innovations: Manageability is a worldwide objective. Developments in green advancements, like energy-effective arrangements and eco-accommodating items, are fundamental. These modern goliaths can lead the way in creating economical choices across enterprises.

Medical care and Biotechnology: The medical care area offers open doors for development, from telemedicine answers for cutting edge diagnostics. Aditya Birla Gathering's emphasis on medical care and drugs positions it to lead there.

High level Assembling: Creating progressed fabricating processes, like 3D printing and computerization, can upgrade proficiency and item quality. This can be especially significant in ventures like aviation and car.

Computer based intelligence and AI: Man-made reasoning (artificial intelligence) and AI have applications in a large number of areas, including money, medical care, and client support. Developments in man-made intelligence can prompt more customized benefits and further developed navigation.

Space and Aviation: The space and aviation ventures offer potential for advancement. With expanding revenue in space investigation and satellite innovation, these aggregates can put resources into related developments and exploration.

Worldwide Effect:

Worldwide Extension: The worldwide development of these combinations can fundamentally affect global business sectors. Goodbye Gathering's obtaining of Panther Land Wanderer, Dependence Ventures' worldwide presence, and Aditya Birla Gathering's worldwide tasks exhibit their impact on a worldwide scale.

Mechanical Headways: These modern monsters are strategically situated to drive innovative progressions. Goodbye Consultancy Administrations, for example, assumes a vital part in the worldwide IT administrations area. The developments created by these combinations can lastingly affect innovation and strategic policies around the world.

Ecological Initiative: As the world looks to address natural difficulties, these modern monsters' obligation to maintainability can set worldwide benchmarks. Their interests in sustainable power, eco-accommodating arrangements, and dependable waste administration can motivate comparable activities by organizations around the world.

Production network Enhancement: The streamlining of supply chains by these combinations can internationally affect coordinated factors and exchange. Smoothing out supply chains can lessen costs and work on the effectiveness of worldwide exchange organizations.

Monetary Administrations and Incorporation: Extending monetary administrations can advance monetary consideration on a worldwide scale. Aditya Birla Gathering and different aggregates can offer monetary types of assistance to underserved locales, adding to financial turn of events and dependability.

Broadcast communications and Availability: The development of broadcast communications and network administrations by these modern goliaths can connect computerized separates and elevate worldwide admittance to data and correspondence.

Social Obligation: The social obligation drives embraced by these combinations, like schooling, medical care, and provincial turn of events, can have a positive worldwide effect. Their obligation to social causes can rouse comparable activities by partnerships around the world.

Innovative work Joint efforts: Joint efforts in innovative work with worldwide accomplices can prompt developments with worldwide ramifications. The innovative headways and arrangements created through such joint efforts can have extensive impacts.

8.3 Closing thoughts on the dynamic evolution of India's industrial landscape.

The unique development of India's modern scene mirrors an excursion of change, strength, and variation. India's modern monsters, like Goodbye Gathering, Dependence Enterprises, and Aditya Birla Gathering, play had a focal impact in this development, adding to the country's financial development and worldwide impact. As we think about the always evolving scene, a few critical experiences and shutting contemplations arise.

1. **Transformation and Versatility:**
   The capacity of India's modern monsters to adjust to changing conditions and display flexibility despite challenges has been a sign of their prosperity. From Goodbye Gathering's venture into new businesses and its obligation to development to Dependence Enterprises' fast computerized change and broadening, these aggregates have reliably shown their nimbleness. This versatility has permitted them to flourish in the midst of changing business sector elements and financial movements.

2. **Worldwide Desires and Global Reach:**
   India's modern monsters have not restricted their aspirations to the homegrown market. They have looked to lay out a worldwide presence, growing their tasks and impact past India's lines. Goodbye Gathering's securing of global brands like Panther Land Meanderer, Dependence Businesses' presence in different areas around the world, and Aditya Birla Gathering's worldwide activities embody their worldwide reach. This worldwide viewpoint has situated them as persuasive players on the worldwide stage.

3. **Development and Innovation Initiative:**
   Development and innovative headway have been key drivers of development and seriousness for these combinations. Organizations like Goodbye Consultancy Administrations (TCS) have cut out a specialty in the worldwide IT administrations area, while

Dependence Businesses' emphasis on computerized administrations and web based business has disturbed India's media communications and retail areas. The obligation to innovative work and the reception of state of the art advances have empowered these modern monsters to remain at the bleeding edge of industry patterns.

4. **Manageability and Ecological Obligation:**

The acknowledgment of natural manageability as really important is a characterizing component of India's modern scene. The shift toward environmentally friendly power arrangements and eco-accommodating practices by Goodbye Power, Aditya Birla Gathering, and different aggregates mirrors their obligation to decreasing their carbon impression and adding to worldwide natural objectives. As environmental change concerns escalate, these endeavors are characteristic of their part in progressing maintainable practices.

5. **Social Obligation and Effect Drives:**

India's modern monsters have recognized their social obligation and the effect they can make on society. Drives by Goodbye Gathering in schooling, medical care, and provincial turn of events, for example, highlight their obligation to working on the personal satisfaction for millions. This emphasis on friendly effect lines up with the more extensive worldwide pattern of corporate social obligation and features their endeavors to reward the networks they serve.

6. **Difficulties and Vulnerabilities:**

While what's in store seems promising, it isn't without difficulties and vulnerabilities. These modern monsters face worldwide monetary vulnerabilities, mechanical disturbances, changing administrative conditions, and the need to stay serious in a quick developing scene. Exploring these difficulties requires proceeded with versatility, risk the executives, and key premonition.

7. **The Job of Government Strategies:**

   Government strategies and drives play had a crucial impact in molding the development of India's modern scene. The "Make in India" crusade, "Atmanirbhar Bharat," and different approaches have given open doors and motivators to homegrown assembling, confidence, and the development of the confidential area. Coordinated efforts and organizations between these aggregates and the public authority have been instrumental in accomplishing normal monetary objectives.

8. **Potential for Coordinated effort and Organizations:**

   Joint effort and associations are instrumental in encouraging advancement and tending to worldwide difficulties. By working with different organizations, research establishments, new businesses, and worldwide associations, India's modern monsters can additionally drive innovative progressions, supportable practices, and financial turn of events. Such organizations can be an impetus for development and advancement.

9. **The Force of Ability and Human Resources:**

   The achievement and advancement of these combinations rely upon drawing in, holding, and creating top ability. A talented and different labor force is fundamental for driving exploration, improvement, and functional greatness. Putting resources into ability improvement and cultivating a culture of development is urgent for guaranteeing future achievement.

10. **The Worldwide Effect and Impact:**

India's modern monsters are ready to have a worldwide effect. Their mechanical developments, ecological authority, monetary administrations, and social obligation drives can rouse comparable activities by organizations around the world. As India keeps on arising as a conspicuous worldwide player, these combinations assume a critical part in molding the country's worldwide impact and monetary development.

All things considered, the unique development of India's modern scene is a demonstration of the versatility, flexibility, and responsibility of its modern goliaths. Their process has been set apart by development, development, and a worldwide standpoint. As they keep on adjusting to changing business sector elements, cultivate development, and address squeezing worldwide difficulties, they are strategically set up to leave an enduring heritage in the domains of innovation, manageability, and social effect.

The modern scene's future isn't without challenges, yet these combinations have shown their capacity to explore vulnerability and arise more grounded. With an emphasis on manageability, development, and worldwide reach, they are ready to shape India's modern future and add to worldwide monetary and mechanical headways. The excursion of development proceeds, and these modern goliaths are at the very front, driving India's change on a worldwide stage.